Goal
Directed
Project
Management

Goal Directed Project Management

SECOND EDITION

Erling S Andersen
Kristoffer V Grude
Tor Haug

**Introduced and edited
by Terry Gibbons**

Translated by Roberta Wiig

Coopers
& Lybrand

**KOGAN
PAGE**

YOURS TO HAVE AND TO HOLD

BUT NOT TO COPY

First published in Norway in 1984 by NKI-forlaget

© Erling S Andersen, Kristoffer V Grude, Tor Haug, 1984

Harback edition first published in Great Britain in 1987 by Kogan Page Ltd.

Reprinted in paperback in 1988

Second edition 1995

Reprinted 1995

Kogan Page Limited
120 Pentonville Road
London N1 9JN

© Erling S Andersen, Kristoffer V Grude and Tor Haug, 1987, 1988, 1995

British Library Cataloguing in Publication Data
A CIP record for this book is available from the British Library.
ISBN 0 7494 1389 1

Typeset by Saxon Graphics Ltd, Derby
Printed and bound in Great Britain by Biddles Ltd, Guildford and King's Lynn
Translated from Norwegian by Roberta Wiig
Introduced and edited by Terry Gibbons

Contents

Foreword to the Third Norwegian Edition

This is a book on project management with a difference. It does not, for example, discuss traditional network planning such as PERT or CPM. Instead it provides a new way of looking at project tasks. 'Goal Directed Project Management' (GDPM) – the method and the philosophy on which it is based – has been developed by the authors, and each has made his individual mark on it.

Development has taken place over a long period of time. Many organisations and individuals have helped to develop the method. Work started at the beginning of the 1970s. For the last ten years we have advised and trained many Norwegian businesses in GDPM. We have taught the method for many years at Norwegian educational institutions.

Through Coopers & Lybrand the method has been disseminated to other countries. We are proud that the book has been published in many languages (Swedish, Danish, Dutch, English and Italian), and it looks as though more will follow.

The book is in its third Norwegian edition. It was first published in 1984, the second edition appearing in 1987. We continue to advocate the central concepts of milestones and responsibility charts in project management. We have described these areas even more precisely as a result of feedback from earlier readers and users of the method. In addition we discuss further how we can achieve high quality in project work and develop a good project culture within a business. We have included a new chapter on objective breakdown structure – an aid in the clarification of the project objectives.

This third edition presents a further improvement of the method, but it is subject to continual refinement and we continue to value your suggestions and opinions.

The authors
Oslo
April 1993

About the Authors

Erling S Andersen is professor of information science at the University of Bergen, Norway. He is also adjunct professor at the Norwegian School of Management, Oslo. He has written several books and scientific papers on subjects such as project management, management in general and computer-based information systems. He is a former president of the Norwegian Computer Society.

Kristoffer Grude has recently established his own management consultancy. He is a former managing director and partner of Coopers & Lybrand Consulting, Norway, in which capacity he obtained broad international experience. He has experience as project manager for a wide variety of small and large projects, as well as training experience.

Tor Haug is an independent consultant, being an expert on IT-strategies, organisational re-engineering and project management. He has more than 30 years of working experience with management and corporate development. He is a former partner of Coopers & Lybrand Consulting, Norway. He has also served as president of the Norwegian Computer Society.

Terry Gibbons is a partner in Change Management consulting practice of Coopers & Lybrand in the UK where he has advised many clients in both the public and private sectors on the implementation of major projects, ranging from the introduction of new systems and technology to the acquisition and reorganisation of businesses.

Preface to the Second English Edition

Goal Directed Project Management is probably the most influential book ever written on the subject of project management. Through its translation into English and other languages it has reached a very large audience throughout the world. I first became involved in the method when Coopers & Lybrand decided to adopt GDPM as its standard approach to project management throughout Europe. I was struck by the foresight that the authors showed in their emphasis on the human and organisational side of projects. In this, they anticipated by a number of years the now well-established science of 'change management'. Goal Directed Project Management (GDPM), in its central focus on developing understanding, involvement and commitment amongst those involved, is a key ingredient in managing successful and lasting change.

The authors touch upon this intimate relationship between managing change and the key ideas of GDPM at many points throughout the book, but I feel it is worthwhile to explore this more fully to give GDPM its appropriate place in management thinking. In Coopers & Lybrand, we have adopted the following as a working definition of change management. It is:

> The process of aligning an organisation's people and culture with changes in business strategy, organisational structure, systems and processes which results in:
>
> ❑ ownership of and commitment to change;
> ❑ sustained and measurable improvement;
> ❑ improved capability to manage future change.

The whole concept of PSO projects rests on the belief that one needs to develop people and the organisation in alignment with the 'systems', the concrete aspects of the business change, so we do not need to look far to find our first point of contact. I have already referred to GDPM's vital emphasis on ownership and commitment.

As for sustained and measurable improvement, GDPM starts with a business or organisational goal and directs the whole management process towards the achievement of that goal. Projects have, in fact, no other rationale or justification and, to be worthwhile, the goal must be measurable and sustainable.

The third requirement is that the way we manage change should lead to an improved capability to manage future change. Here, I have seen GDPM have a very remarkable effect, perhaps because the approach is accessible not only to specialists but to all the participants in a project and insists that they be involved in the management process. In a number of cases, we have introduced GDPM in the context of a particular project and have quickly seen the language, concepts and tools gain wide currency in the organisation. As a result, the general level of awareness and competence in project management has been raised across a broad cross-section of people.

Over the last three years, Coopers & Lybrand have developed an approach to managing business change which has three main elements:

- a clearly articulated vision of what needs to change and why;
- an analysis of the behavioural dimensions and risks of change and a planned response to them;
- a systematic approach to the management of complex change programmes.

It should be clear from the above that it was natural for us to choose GDPM as the core of our programme management approach, but there are significant parallels in the other two elements as well. In developing the change vision we have drawn heavily on the work of Burke and Litwin.[1] They propose a systems model for organisational performance incorporating 12 key variables – leadership, culture, organisational structure, management practices and so on – which can form the basis for the vision of the future business. In the concept of 'Objective Breakdown Structure', new in this edition of the book, I see the opportunity to incorporate these organisational variables explicitly into project objectives.

In managing the behavioural aspects of change, we have used the work of Conner[2] who identifies a number of behavioural patterns in undertaking change and proposes how the organisation should best mobilise its resources to carry it through. One of the most important principles concerns how certain key roles need to be recognised and carried out effectively. Not surprisingly, the most influential role is that of 'sponsor' and Conner spells out very clearly what sponsors have to do to sustain business change. This principle that key roles need to be established and responsibilities and relationships spelt out is exactly reflected in the responsibility chart. Together, these ideas give precision to the concept of sponsorship, which project managers have known from time immemorial was vital for success but have often had difficulty in giving shape to.

Conner draws out many other principles such as the need to surface and manage resistance to change, to build commitment, to focus staff on a common goal and to build their capability to work together. I believe GDPM has something valuable to contribute in all these areas, too.

In summary, then, we greeted the original book as a clear expression of much of what we thought was important in project management and, over the years, have adopted it as our standard approach. In 1993, we established a European Project Management Centre of Excellence based on the principles of GDPM, drawing together the experience and expertise of five participating countries – Norway, the Netherlands, the United Kingdom, Belgium and Denmark. The Director of this Centre of Excellence is Jacques J.A.M. Reijniers, a partner in the Utrecht office of Coopers & Lybrand, Netherlands. More recently, we have seen the synergy between GDPM and the emerging discipline of change management and this has reinforced our commitment to it. The new edition extends the ideas of the original book and supplements them with some new and illuminating examples, but I was not disappointed to find that the core ideas remain essentially the same. It is a worthwhile development of a significant book.

Terry Gibbons
Coopers & Lybrand, Birmingham
February 1995

References

1 Burke, W W and Litwin, G H (1989) *A Causal Model of Organisational Performance,* annual of developing human resources, San Diego, University Associates.
2 Conner, D F (1993), *Managing at the Speed of Change,* New York, Villard Books.

List of Figures

1
Introduction

OUTLINE

This book deals with project management. We discuss the requirements for successful projects, we present methods and tools which increase significantly the probability of success, and we show how a project can be guided towards achieving its goals.

The book is written for both project managers and those participating in projects. Throughout the book we have used 'he' and related words purely for convenience. There are many female project managers and, therefore, 'she' is implied equally throughout. The book requires no special previous knowledge of project work.

Much project literature concerns technical projects. Examples are often taken from construction of bridges, roads, airports or oil platforms. We have a broader perspective. We are interested in what we call PSO projects. PSO stands for people, system and organisation; PSO projects are projects where development of a 'system' (for example, a physical product or object) and development of people and organisations will occur simultaneously. Most projects have, or should have, this objective. Therefore it is wise to develop a 'PSO way of thinking' in project management. In the first chapter we discuss the nature of a PSO project in detail.

In Chapter 2 we look at the characteristic features of a project, the conditions that make project work essentially different from the daily routines in a line organisation. A discussion of these dissimilarities will aid an understanding of special management problems in project work. Special tools are also required in project management.

We deal with conditions that we know from experience create problems in project work. We refer to these conditions as 'pitfalls'. The discussion of pitfalls in Chapter 3 further illustrates the need for special methods and tools in project work.

Against this background we present the specific methods and tools of Goal Directed Project Management (GDPM). We take up global planning (Chapter 4) and organisation (Chapter 5). Thereafter we discuss detailed planning and organisation (Chapter 6). Control (Chapter 7) is an integral part of project management.

We discuss what role the different categories of project participants should play in a project and we look at the importance of good interaction between them (Chapter 8).

We discuss ways of achieving quality in project work (Chapter 9). With the help of what we call an objective breakdown structure, we discuss how we can further clarify the objectives of a project (Chapter 10). This is also an important aspect of improving the quality of project work.

In conclusion, we show that the methods of GDPM can also be used in other contexts, and we look at what role project management can play in work towards quality certification of a business (Chapter 11).

Figure 1.1 gives a schematic presentation of GDPM. The figure shows which tools we recommend for the planning, organisation and control of tasks. Chapters 4–7 are thus a basic course in how to manage projects and how to use the recommended tools.

The project mandate provides the background for the project and shows what its goal is. The objective breakdown structure assists in setting the boundaries of the project and defining the goals precisely. The milestone plan is a global plan for project progress, with checkpoints in the form of milestones to be achieved. The principle responsibility chart shows the division of work between the different parties involved in managing the project. The project responsibility chart shows who is responsible for attaining the different milestones. The activity responsibility chart describes in more detail who should work on the different activities necessary for reaching a milestone. It also shows when

Task Level	Project planning	Project organisation	Project control
Global level (project level)	Objective breakdown structure Project mandate Milestone plan	Principle responsibility chart Project responsibility chart	Milestone report Project report
Detail level (activity level)	Activity responsibility chart		Activity report

Figure 1.1 *Overview of Goal Directed Project Management*

the different activities must be performed. The milestone report shows where the project is in relation to the milestone plan. A project (responsibility chart) report reveals if the responsibility chart is kept to. An activity report is used to prepare a detailed report of project work progress.

ABOUT PSO PROJECTS

The concept of PSO development was used originally within the field of information technology. It is based on countless experiences with the implementation of computer systems. These experiences taught us that successful implementation requires more than a concern with the technical development of the computer system. It must always be accompanied by planned development, both of the affected personnel and of the relationships of responsibility and authority in the organisation. This is necessary in order to achieve the required benefits of systems development, and to prevent it from having negative effects on people and the organisation.

It is a frequent mistake when introducing a new computer system to overemphasise the technical work. The development of people and organisation necessary to enable the computer system to function well is either totally neglected or paid insufficient attention. The PSO concept reminds us of the importance of balancing all three elements.

We have found the PSO approach to be extremely useful in other types of project work. Projects often involve the building or installation of a physical product. It is very easy to become so preoccupied with this that the training and motivation of the people who will use this product is forgotten. It is easy to overlook the fact that innovations also facilitate completely new forms of organisation.

Therefore, we also use the PSO concept in project planning. The 'S', however, must be given a broad interpretation. It stands for technical aspects of the project. It often represents what we can 'touch and feel' in the project. In a product development project, the new product forms the 'S'; in a construction project, the new building is the 'S'; in a merger project, the newly merged company is the 'S'. Using the PSO concept requires a little thought and extra effort, but the reward is a broader view of what the project involves. The need to consider people and organisation is not forgotten. It forces one to think through consequences and possibilities in fields other than the purely technical.

The most common failing in project work is to focus too strongly on the technical content. In typical organisational development projects the situation is the reverse. These are solely concerned with developing people in the organisation and relationships between them. There is too little emphasis on developing systems (eg routines and procedures) which will support the changes required in the organisation.

PSO projects are thus projects where the result should be a composite 'product'; goals should be achieved in all 'P', 'S' and 'O'.

Another important and characteristic aspect of project work is the extent to which people involved in the project (who will use the results) are invited to participate in the work. One extreme is the purely specialist project. In such projects all the work is performed by specialists without any form of cooperation or consultation with the end users. An example may be a technical installation according to specific instructions, or an expert report by two or three technical specialists. Here there is no place for user cooperation or any opening for new approaches to problems and solutions which may follow from cooperation with the users.

The other extreme is the purely process-oriented project. Here little or no consideration is given to planning the technical outcome. On the contrary, everyone is encouraged to become involved, and the project is allowed to be dominated by whatever problems and possibilities the participants see as being most important at any given time. The process itself (the interaction between people and what it leads to) determines the progress of the project. We have illustrated these types of projects on a scale (Figure 1.2).

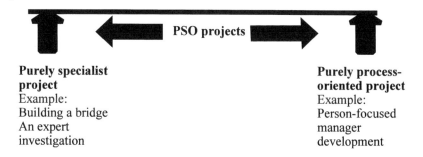

Purely specialist project
Example:
Building a bridge
An expert
investigation

Purely process-oriented project
Example:
Person-focused
manager
development

Figure 1.2 *Different types of projects*

It is our firm belief that all PSO projects are 'mixed' projects. They contain elements both from the process-oriented approach and from the specialist project.

PSO projects often have profound consequences for the business and the people within it. It is important that the people concerned become involved in the project and that they are given an opportunity to influence it. Their attitude to and understanding of the result produced depends to a great extent on the manner in which they have participated in the project activities.

However, PSO projects can also contain complex technical elements, where a successful result depends entirely on using expertise and using methods and technology with great precision. In one and the same PSO project some activities may be very highly process-orientated while others may be highly expert-dominated.

GOAL DIRECTED PROJECT MANAGEMENT

This book, then, deals with the management of PSO projects. It is essential in PSO projects that there be a balance between development of the 'system' (the 'object' to be constructed) and development of people and organisation. Work will typically consist of process-oriented and specialist-oriented parts.

Management consists of organising the use of resources and the work towards goals. Both the organisation and the work towards goals are complex, particularly when providing a product which is *not* purely technical but a composite result. In a PSO project the result consists of some technology (which may be physically inspected), but also of people with new knowledge and attitudes and of an organisation and environment within which the system and the people can function well.

The responsibility for the project achieving its goals does not rest solely with the formal project manager. Everyone who can contribute in one way or another to the project achieving the desired goals is responsible for the project result.

In PSO projects goal management is absolutely essential. One must not lose sight of the composite goal. It is simpler when constructing a bridge or building a house. The goal is concrete – the bridge or the house. With PSO projects the goal is more abstract. It is easy to be preoccupied with the more concrete or technical aspects of the project, the completion date, for example, rather than with the composite goal.

In order to underline how important it is to remain continually aware of the composite goal, we have called the book and the method we present 'Goal Directed Project Management' (GDPM).

The method contains procedures and tools which support project management. It shows how to organise resources in an organisationally complex situation. It shows how to set goals, and break each goal down into controllable intermediate goals, and how to divide work tasks into many parts and then monitor them so that the intermediate goals are achieved on the way towards a completed project.

2

Project Characteristics

In order to understand a project, consider it in the context of the organisation that undertakes it. The organisation can be a company, a voluntary organisation or a branch of the civil service. These all aim to produce certain goods or provide services. One company produces chocolate, another aluminium products; some organisations educate and do research; still others offer health services.

Each organisation is structurally tailor-made for the type of production or activity in which it engages. This means that each worker has set tasks, tasks which must be performed repeatedly. This applies to everyone working in the organisation, from those on the factory floor or the hospital ward, to those who manage the business. The manager's day is not as structured as that of the workers lower down in the business, but the manager also has set tasks, such as the development of strategy plans and budgets, preparation for board meetings, and so forth. Everyone in the business has what we call repetitive tasks.

Now and then, however, tasks arise with which the business is not equipped to deal. These are tasks of a non-recurring type. They have not been done previously and will not be done again in the foreseeable future. Examples might be moving to new locations, holding an anniversary celebration or finding opportunities for entering the German market. Each of these tasks involve many people in the business, yet it does not belong in any one place in the organisation.

In cases like these the project approach is relevant. It is an alternative to performing the task within the traditional organisational structure. We will refer to the traditional organisation as the base organisation. We establish a project to carry out a determined task because the base organisation is not adequately organised to perform it.

In Figure 2.1 we have summarised the characteristic features of a project. You will find such a list in most textbooks on project work. The description in Figure 2.1 is often used as a definition of a project.

A project
- is a unique task
- is designed to attain a specific result
- requires a variety of resources
- is limited in time

Figure 2.1 *Characteristic features of a project*

Below we make more detailed comments on the different characteristic features of a project and indicate what is important from the management perspective.

A UNIQUE TASK

One reason for organising a task as a project is exactly that it is a unique, one-time task. If it is a task which will be performed repeatedly, it is more natural to hand it over to the line organisation.

The problem with a unique task is that no one has been through it previously. Therefore at the outset one does not know in detail which activities need to be performed and consequently one does not have a detailed blueprint for how to proceed in order to achieve the desired results. An analysis must be made of what work needs to be done and in what order. Project work must therefore be planned by a method other than that used for line tasks.

It is important to emphasise that a project task is also new to specialists – even if they have performed the same type of work previously – as it is to be performed in an unfamiliar area, in a new environment and with new people.

A person who has been a project manager for a PSO project in one business cannot copy the activities from that project into another context. The change process to be undertaken will be different because it deals with different people in a different environment. The activities may consequently be totally different, even if they are aiming towards the same result.

A consultant may have been a project manager responsible for implementing a computerised wage system in a company and have done an excellent job. That same consultant, however, may not succeed in implementing the same system into another business. Many wonder why this is so. It may be because the consultant uses the same approach regardless of the people and the environment he is working with, which reveals that he has not understood the importance of the 'P' and 'O' elements of the project. He has not understood that he is confronted with a new task, for which new plans must be made.

ATTAINMENT OF A SPECIFIC RESULT

A project is established to perform a specific task in order to achieve a specific result. The task can vary greatly from project to project. One project may be to construct a bridge over a river, another the implementation of a computer system in the accounting function of a company, a third an investigation of the consequences of moving part of a company to another geographical location.

It is very important that a project is formed to achieve a specific result. It is equally important to point out that there may be very different emphases on process-oriented and specialist-oriented work in order to achieve that result (see the discussion in Chapter 1). In a PSO project, the process-oriented elements are very important. The work of developing relationships between the participants and attitudes towards the task in question is an essential part of the project.

A PSO project is a change process, a process that changes people's working environment as well as their understanding of the organisation of which they are part. Consequently, project management is change management.

It is a completely different, highly sensitive and difficult management task compared with the one which a line manager usually has. A line manager primarily manages tasks that are constantly repeated each day, week or year, and the people involved are aware of the effect of these actions.

One often encounters the notion that project work really consists only of specialist work. This creates particular problems for a project manager. In such cases it may be difficult for him to obtain acceptance for the importance of the work on the process-orientated elements. Often they are the most time consuming parts of the project.

REQUIRES A VARIETY OF RESOURCES

This section deals with several types of management problems. First, particularly in businesses that are not accustomed to working with projects, it is difficult to achieve an understanding of the resources required for a successful project. There are several reasons why line organisations are reluctant to commit resources:

❑ They hope that staff can participate in project work on top of their regular job, without any reduction in their original responsibilities.
❑ They do not understand why the project should take such a long time. (Perhaps because they have no firm grasp of their own use of resources.)
❑ They think they can negotiate a shorter time-frame.
❑ They do not understand that a reduction in resources means a reduction in quality, and that a reduction in quality creates problems at the next stage.
❑ They believe that a lack of resources will resolve itself along the way.

Problems are intensified if the project is highly process-oriented. It is even more difficult to gain acceptance for the time and effort required for this type of work. One can understand to a certain extent that technical work requires resources because one can see the physical processes. With process-oriented projects, however, line managers often have a limited understanding of what it takes to achieve good results, and this makes it difficult to have a realistic discussion of resource requirements. (We are not saying here that all 'P' and 'O' activities necessarily take a long time. Some situations require a long period of development, but it often takes a surprisingly short time to obtain much better results. A few days of concentrated effort on the 'P' and 'O' areas, therefore, gives significant results compared with neglecting these issues.)

The second point is that even if there is a real understanding of the need for resources, there are often problems releasing the required people at the required time. Usually people in the base organisation are committed on a full-time basis to other tasks and cannot participate in the project unless these other tasks are covered one way or another. This situation creates special management problems.

With regard to resources, most businesses are geared up for an average workload. This means that the business is understaffed during periods with a heavy workload, while idle during 'quiet periods'. Attention should be paid to this when staffing a project.

The third management problem is that a project includes people from different backgrounds having different expertise and experience. That a project brings together people with different skills is precisely the point of project management; project tasks are solved by precisely this method. These people have probably not worked together previously and this is a challenge for the project manager. The people are not necessarily difficult to handle, but their varied backgrounds, expectations and ambitions can impede the success of a project if no effort is made to form a 'team'. Time must be devoted to providing opportunities for project members to get to know each other, enabling them to draw on each other's strengths later on.

TIME CONSTRAINTS

A typical feature of a project is that there is a fixed completion date. There is often a strong focus on this date and the success of the project will be judged on whether or not the project is completed by then.

A task subject to time limits is not a feature special to project work, but the focus on the completion date is stronger here than in many other cases. In a line organisation with repetitive tasks there are additional opportunities to make up time if the deadline is exceeded. There is no such possibility in project work. A black shadow always hangs over a project which does not meet its deadlines.

Problems are intensified for project management if the completion date for the project is set on a fairly arbitrary basis only considering the technical aspects of the project.

We will discuss later how to set reasonable completion dates for projects, but we must already point out now that it is psychologically unsound to connect all expectations for change to a specific date. If the result has not been achieved by this date, there is a sharp drop in motivation in the line organisation. Instead of linking expectations to a single date, many intermediate results should be planned, to be achieved during the course of the project. In this way, the 'big day' crisis situation is defused.

PROJECT MANAGEMENT

We have discussed above the characteristic features of a project and stressed the fact that it gives rise to particular leadership and management problems. Figure 2.2 is a reformulation of Figure 2.1. The new figure illustrates the particular problems presented by projects.

A project
- involves new and unknown tasks
- leads to a change in people's daily work or living conditions
- requires the right people at the right time, but staff of different backgrounds who are not used to working together
- is subject to a strict deadline

Figure 2.2 *Characteristic features of a project (reformulated)*

A PSO project implements change, which is difficult in itself. The change is to occur within a stated period of time. It is an unknown task for many of those involved. Resources will be required that in many cases are not available or belong to other managers, organisationally speaking. It is not surprising that this is a difficult task.

A project requires the establishment of an organisational structure and that work within this structure be managed with the assistance of specific methods and tools. Project management means organising, planning, and controlling the project (see Figure 2.3).

A recipe for good project management can, of course, draw on our general knowledge of management, but the special conditions associated with project work also mean that project management requires special knowledge and methods.

```
                    Project Management
                    –   Planning
                    –   Organising
                    –   Controlling
```

Figure 2.3 *Subsidiary tasks in project management*

3

Pitfalls in Project Management

'The key to being a successful project manager is being able to forecast accurately the work to be done and the time required to do it.' This fallacy is the first pitfall from which many more arise. You cannot solve management problems with mathematics alone. There are several preconditions for the success or failure of a project, and good forecasting is just one of them.

In this chapter we discuss some of the pitfalls that can occur on the road to a successful project. The pitfalls are grouped under five headings:

- ❏ Foundations of the project.
- ❏ Planning of the project.
- ❏ Organisation of the project.
- ❏ Control of the project.
- ❏ Execution of the project work.

The first of these headings concerns the basic assumptions underlying the project and its position within the company, the next three are about project management, and the last is about the quality of professional work being undertaken.

CRACKS IN THE FOUNDATIONS

We start with the position the project has in the company which is undertaking it, and the relationships between the senior executives and the project management. In particular, we consider the degree to which the executives support the project. The executives' attitude and the preliminary work provide the foundation for the project. If there are cracks in this foundation, the total project will suffer.

We consider the possible flaws in the foundations under the two areas introduced above:

❑ Insufficient support for the project.
❑ Poor project definition.

Insufficient support for the project

Two dangers await the project manager who has little or no support from the company or its executives:

❑ The project plans are not aligned with the business plans.
❑ The principles and policies of project work are not defined.

Unaligned project and business plans

There must be a close correlation between the plans for the general development of the business and the development desired from the project. The project must fit into the overall plans for the company, with the projects goals and corporate objectives in harmony. Furthermore, the project's activities must be given adequate priority by the company. Unfortunately, it is not uncommon to find work initiated without any connection to other business plans. This is often true with new computer systems, which can have a major impact on the people, systems and organisation of a company.

If a PSO project is not evaluated in the larger context, a conflict can easily occur between the direction in which the company's management wants the business to develop, and the way in which the project work contributes to that development.

There is no doubt who will be the loser in this tug of war. No leadership nor project management method can save a project that has no support within the company. A project without steady support from the top can end dramatically. When the company's management suddenly realise that the project is heading for a collision with more important plans, they will just pull the plug.

However, it is more common for management to have a half-hearted attitude towards the project. The project is choked slowly by the lack of necessary resources and decisions. In all discussions about resources the project invariably loses due to its lack of support. The project continues but without the hope of reaching its original goals. People step in to do the work which should have been done by others. For example, in an IT project, programmers do jobs which should have been done by the users, because the users give insufficient priority to the project and do not provide resources for it. The result is a data system without user support.

A project manager responsible for a project which lacks sufficient support is in a compromised position. Should he continue with the project? Or should he accept the inevitable, and withdraw from further participation? The project manager is torn between loyalty for the task he has been given, and consideration for his own career. Poor project results will usually reflect on the project manager, even if caused by factors beyond his control.

The creation of a project independent of the corporate plans is the most dramatic pitfall because, more than anything else, it is the most likely to ensure the failure of the project.

Undefined principles and policies of project work

Well defined principles and policies for project work create the climate which ensures that a project functions well. Questions that should be answered in the general project guidelines include:

- What is the corporate and line management's responsibility for the project work?
- Who is responsible for committing resources?
- What are the policies for making resources available?
- What are the tools and methods to be used for the management of the project?
- How are co-ordination and co-operation to be achieved?

If these general guidelines for project work are not defined in advance, valuable project time will be lost discussing principles that should have been clarified at the outset, which will reduce the project's momentum. A project is based on a certain understanding of the way people are to co-operate. If that understanding proves to be wrong, the project members will cease to work in harmony, and their efficiency will drop.

Poor project definition

There are three consequences of not precisely defining the project from the outset:

- ❏ The goals for the project are imprecise.
- ❏ The limits of the scope of the project are not set.
- ❏ The levels of ambition for changes to people, systems and organisation are not in balance with the new technology to be introduced.

Imprecise project goals

The floundering of many projects can be traced back to unclear or imprecise goals. Not enough effort has been put into defining the problems that the project should solve.

There are four phases to problem solving:

- ❏ decision-making;
- ❏ decision-taking;
- ❏ implementation;
- ❏ monitoring.

The first phase consists of defining the problem and generating alternative solutions, the second of selecting from those solutions. It is an unfortunate human tendency to spend insufficient time on the first phase, racing on to discuss possible solutions before the problem is properly defined. Another failing, which is equally undesirable, is to cycle endlessly between decision-making and decision-taking, so avoiding implementation.

When selecting a new computer system, project members quickly enter a discussion on technical matters, before being clear on the change the new system is meant to achieve. Concrete activities, such as programming, assume priority over abstract activities such as deciding what should be achieved.

Undefined limits of scope

A related pitfall is failing to define properly the scope of the project. Consequently, the project solves the wrong problem, or the project members waste time doing work that is not their responsibility. This pitfall is avoided by having a thorough milestone plan and a clear responsibility chart.

Unbalanced levels of ambition

A PSO project results in both technical and procedural change. The technical change might be a new computer system or a new manufacturing facility. The procedural change will be the new knowledge, new assignments, and new managers required to operate the new system or facility.

There is often a tendency in the specification of a project to overemphasise the technical aspects and ignore the organisational aspects. People find it easier to imagine the concrete, technical tasks rather than the abstract, organisational ones.

The project manager must maintain balanced goals. He must ensure that the technology introduced is the right response to the needs of the company, and that the company is left with the right people, with the right skills and adequate systems to use the technology. The process of milestone planning gives him a method to focus the attention of project members on both the technical and procedural activities.

To avoid pitfalls the project manager needs methods and tools which force him and the project members to spend time clarifying the aims of the project. The milestone plan fulfils this role. However, the task of milestone planning can be made easier by having the problem to be solved defined in a specification or project statement of user requirements. We discuss this further in Chapter 4.

PITFALLS IN PLANNING

The following elements can create pitfalls in planning:

- ❑ The planning level is uniform; the plan contains too much detail for some users, and too little for others.
- ❑ The planning tools are unwieldy.

- ❏ The planning range is psychologically unsound.
- ❏ The planning method discourages creativity, and encourages bureaucracy.
- ❏ The planning estimates of time and cost are over-optimistic.
- ❏ The planning of resources overestimates their competence and capacity.
- ❏ The project calendar omits lost time.
- ❏ The plan omits activities.

The planning level is uniform

The most serious pitfall in planning is to select a planning level that is uniform and consequently impractical. Making a plan at one level, we must either choose a plan that is too broad in scope, with insufficient detail, or choose one that is too detailed, and hence does not map the achievement of goals throughout the project.

Project managers fall more often into the latter trap, planning the project activity by activity. They find that as soon as they start the project more information becomes available, so some activities are no longer required, while new activities are required. The project manager is sucked into a spiral of planning and replanning. He ceases to manage and the plan loses credibility.

It is not practical to use a detailed plan for reporting to senior managers, or the user. They are interested in whether or not the project will achieve its goals, and they cannot see this in the mass of detailed activities. They need an overview, the milestone plan, which shows them whether or not the project is on target. If a milestone is missed, then they may want additional information, to show what corrective action has been taken. While the project is on target, they need only to be shown that it is.

Alternatively, a plan that is too broad in scope cannot be used to communicate with project staff. If the tasks are too large, progress cannot be measured at regular intervals. There is a greater chance of a misunderstanding, and the project members doing the wrong work.

Project management requires at least two levels of planning, the milestone plan, and the activity plan. The former is the management level; the latter the task level.

The planning tools are unwieldy

The second pitfall follows from the first. It is common to match a plan that exists only at the detail level with unwieldy planning tools. Many of us have seen networks with thousands of activities. These tools hamper communication rather than enhance it.

At each level the tools used for communicating the plan and reporting progress should be on one, or at most two, sheets of paper. The milestone plan and associated definition of responsibility are on two sheets of paper. Managers cannot be expected to comprehend any more in the time available to them. The activities associated with each milestone are on one sheet of paper. Project members must be able to see their work easily, and not need to trace a tortuous trail through a network with thousands of activities.

The planning range is psychologically unsound

There is a tendency in many projects to focus on a deadline. Too much attention is given to this date. By being concerned only about a point that lies far into the future, the project members can feel that there is plenty of time to do the work. Consequently, the project takes low priority. Alternatively, if Parkinson's law holds, the project members fill the time with ineffective work.

The project manager should set definite targets for the completion of the work. To set short time horizons, the plan must contain goals and activities which are controllable in the short term, and towards which the project members can strive.

The planning method discourages creativity

The fourth pitfall follows from the previous three. If the planning level, tools and range are cumbersome, then the project members will not engage in a creative discussion about the plan.

Likewise, it is important that the language used in the plan must be understandable to people other than the specialist; it must be free of jargon.

Planning should be a group activity, where the relevant parties work together to solve the task in hand. It is in the execution of the task that people should take individual responsibility. Planning should be a democratic process, while project implementation is autocratic. However, it is common for the situation to be reversed. The project manager, or even senior management, plans the work in privacy, then delegates the implementation to the group.

The planning of time and cost are over-optimistic

Over-optimism can arise in two ways:

- ❑ Plans are cut arbitrarily and unrealistically.
- ❑ There is insufficient previous experience against which to judge the work content.

Arbitrary cuts

These might be due to genuine optimism, or lack of realism, depending on your viewpoint. We have worked with companies with detailed methods for estimating the work content and cost of projects. These methods and empirical data are used to plan a project, but then they are overtaken by optimism. The managers look at the estimates, and think they are too high. They presume that it must be possible to do the work more quickly and cheaply. However, if you use estimating methods you must trust them and accept the results, otherwise the effort is wasted.

The other situation, which can lead to this type of self-deception, is when the project must be 'sold' to the base organisation, or to an outside customer. To make the project attractive, the project manager reduces the estimates of work content and cost, and then convinces himself that the new estimates can be achieved. Tragically, they usually cannot.

Insufficient previous experience

A second form of over-optimism is to underestimate the time required to achieve procedural changes. Empirical data exists to estimate the time required for technical activities. For example, we know how long it takes to pour 1000 cubic metres of concrete for a factory foundation, and how long it takes to set. We know how long it takes an average programmer to write 1000 lines of COBOL program.

In contrast, we do not know how long it takes to make a procedural change. We do not know how much resistance to the change there will be, and what mode of change can be adopted. Will it be short and sharp, or require months of persuasion? Further, if the progress of change is dependent on certain decisions being made within the company, it is common to ignore the political factors underlying the decision, and to underestimate the time required.

The result is that insufficient time and resources are given for the procedural tasks. Time is not allowed for people to acquire new attitudes and new knowledge. Critical tasks are done inadequately and must be redone. Resources are wasted.

Over-optimism with projects is dangerous. To avoid this pitfall those who are to be committed to the work must be involved in the planning; those who are responsible for the implementation must be realistic. It is important to consider the time and resources required to achieve the process of change, to unfreeze, to implement the change, and to refreeze the organisation. These resources must be included in the plan.

The planning of resources overestimates their competence and capacity

This pitfall is related to the previous one and can contribute to it. Estimates of time and cost are often based on ideal resources, or ideal circumstances. However, the knowledge and experience of the staff available, and the time they can devote to the project, may be less than ideal. The important point is that the plans must be formulated to take account of the actual constraints.

Further, users are often approached too late to provide resources for the project, or they are asked early enough but without obligation. Thus, when his input is required, the user has not made alternative arrangements, and the resources required are not available.

The project calendar ignores lost time

There is a tendency to plan a project as if the outside world does not exist. However, people become ill, they go on holiday, and they attend courses and seminars. These factors reduce their capacity. Our experience is that the reduction can be as much as 20–30 per cent.

The plan omits activities

Because a project is unique our previous experience cannot tell us in advance all the activities which will be involved. If we attempt at the start to make a list of all the activities, which many people try when they plan at the detail level alone, something is bound to be forgotten. Checklists of activities from previous, similar projects help, but since no two projects are identical they must be used carefully. To overcome this pitfall we suggest later that you adopt a rolling wave approach to activity planning.

PITFALLS IN ORGANISING

The following can create pitfalls in organising:

- ❏ Alternative organisations for the project are not considered.
- ❏ The distribution of responsibility is not defined.
- ❏ The principles of co-operation are unclear.
- ❏ Key resources are not available when required.
- ❏ Key resources are not motivated.
- ❏ Line managers are not committed.
- ❏ Communication is poor.
- ❏ The project manager is a technocrat, rather than a manager, so he cannot delegate, coordinate, and control.

Matrix structures versus bureaucratic structures

When selecting an organisation to manage a project, few people stop to reflect that there may be an alternative to modelling it on the hierarchical, or bureaucratic, structure of the base organisation. It has become so common to adopt a hierarchical structure, with steering committee (or management group), project manager, project groups and reference or consultative groups, that the possibility of a matrix or task structure is ignored. The organisational structure should be chosen to suit the particular project at hand. However, we believe that the task-orientated matrix structure is preferable for most PSO projects. We return to this later, when the different structures are described in more detail.

The traditional hierarchical structure, with a steering committee, project manager, and project groups, is best suited to projects that imitate the base organisation. Such projects are usually large, and have purely technical goals, for example the construction of a bridge or a road. The people working on the project devote their entire time to the project during their involvement. The final users of the product are not involved until during, or after, commissioning. When this structure is adopted, the lines of communication and principles of co-operation will have been well defined and tested by previous practice. This will normally occur in contracting companies, in which project work is the usual role of the base organisation.

For most PSO projects, the matrix structure is appropriate, because project members must divide their time between project work and their normal duties in the base organisation. The definition of the matrix structure must clarify the lines of communication and the principles of co-operation. It can also be used to resolve conflicts of priority between project work and the demands of the base organisation.

Symptoms of inappropriate structure

Many of the pitfalls listed above are symptoms of an inappropriate structure.

The usual consequence of failing to clarify responsibilities and the principles of co-operation is that resources are unavailable when required. The key resources are always people with specialist skills, and they are often the busiest people in a company. Their line managers must agree to release them to the project at the right time. The project manager must use the definition of his structure to obtain this agreement. Lack of the necessary resources will of course delay the project.

The problem is aggravated if line managers do not arrange cover for key personnel, because then they must do their normal work in their spare time or the project will be delayed. With this conflict, it is easy to understand how project members come to dislike the project and to lose motivation. The result of accumulating delays is that the plans made by other managers releasing resources will be upset, and the project will enter a downward spiral.

The line manager's personal objectives can conflict with the project's goals. The project may have been forced on him from higher in the company, or he may be unused to development work. He may not have the energy or ability to attend both to project work and to his daily routines. Faced with this situation, a line manager may sit on the fence, watching the project's progress. The consequence is that he will distance himself from decisions for which he has responsibility until it is too late.

Even if he can understand the line manager's lack of commitment to the project, the project manager must not accept the situation and try to live with it, because a reluctant line manager can kill a project. The project manager must agree with him upon his responsibility to the project. If they cannot agree, the negotiations must be conducted at higher levels in the organisation until the problem is resolved. But remember, if the line manager is to be committed, the problem must be resolved, not stamped on.

The project manager as leader

The last organisational pitfall is the selection of the wrong person as project manager. It is not uncommon to select a good technician, but such people are often not suitable.

We recall the important functions of a project manager: to plan, to organise and to control. A good technocrat will know the technical aspects of the work better than anyone else, but he may have problems delegating. He may believe, quite rightly, that he can do the work better and faster than his staff, and attempt to do so, with catastrophic results. He consequently neglects his managerial responsibilities as he works himself to death on the tasks he has assumed.

Who should be project manager – a technical expert, or a user? This question is irrelevant because the person should be chosen for his leadership qualities rather than his background.

The project manager should be someone who:

- has the time and energy;
- can plan, organise and control the work methodically;
- can inspire others to work.

PITFALLS IN CONTROLLING

Formulating a good plan is the first step in project management, and organising the activities of project members is the second. However, project management is not about running ahead of the project members with the plan. It is about providing collaborative leadership from within the team. Control is an important part of that leadership. Control is:

- reporting progress of the project in relation to the plan;
- analysing variance between progress and the plan;
- taking action to eliminate the variances.

The following can create pitfalls in controlling:

- The project manager and his team do not understand the purpose of control, they do not understand the difference between monitoring and controlling.
- The plan and progress reports are not integrated.
- There is no well defined, formalised communication between project manager and project members.
- The project manager has responsibility, but no formal authority.

The purpose of control

Many people do not understand the purpose of project control. The purpose is not to wield a stick, to apportion blame, or to punish the guilty. The purpose is to monitor progress, and to take corrective action in time.

We must stress the point that control is more than just monitoring and reporting progress. In many projects, control merely means writing a few familiar quotes to the project manager on the current status, or extending some lines on a bar chart to show how far the project has progressed. Perhaps the project manager reads what he gets and then conscientiously files the report, but that is where it ends. Reporting becomes a ritual you do because you are told to, rather than an activity you take seriously. Serious control means evaluating the consequences of deviations from the plan and acting upon them.

Integrating plans and progress reports

To facilitate control, the plan should encourage it. Therefore, we suggest that the reports should be written on the plan, so that the plan is reviewed whenever a report is made. This is not usually the case because plans are structured in such a way that control is an enormous administrative burden. They tend to be voluminous, but do not contain information that allows deviation to be analysed effectively.

The classic example is the large, multi-coloured network with thousands of activities that sometimes adorns a project manager's office. It does not encourage control because:

- It is difficult to judge the effect one activity's going late has on the duration of the project.
- It is impossible to monitor productivity from the productivity of individual activities.
- The assessment of quality is something that is left until the last activity is finished, when it is too late.

The ideal plan invites control, and provides information to the project manager to enable him to exercise it.

Formalised communication

A mistake made by many project managers is not to review formally their staff's progress. For them, reviewing progress consists of striking up a conversation around the coffee machine. However, this kind of unsystematic, informal monitoring is inadequate, and never taken seriously.

It is beneficial to have informal conversations on a project, because it aids creative communication, but for effective control, some communication must occur formally, at regular intervals. Contact should occur at set times, with a predefined format. If not, staff lose respect for the review process and control will be ineffective.

Responsibility with authority

Even if he gets all the above right, the project manager will still be unable to control if he does not have the same formal authority as the equivalent manager in the base organisation from whom he is obtaining resources. If a project member has a conflict of priority between the project manager and his line manager, there is seldom any doubt where his loyalty lies. He will choose his line manager because the line manager pays his salary, and he must work for him when the project is finished.

The project manager is ultimately responsible for achieving the project's goals, and therefore must be given commensurate authority. A project manager with charisma will derive some authority from his personality, called personal power. However, most projects will be managed by average people and what they lack in natural authority, they must be given in terms of positional power. Their authority to control the project must be reflected in the project's organisation.

PITFALLS IN EXECUTION OF PROJECT WORK

In the last four sections we described the pitfalls that can arise in setting the term of reference of a project, and subsequently in planning, organising and controlling it. Professional competence is not enough to ensure success if these managerial details are wrong. Likewise, no amount of administrative aids can ensure success if professional competence is lacking. Both are crucial to success.

To end this discussion of pitfalls, we consider some which can arise in the project work. Many will be unique to a particular professional discipline. However, the following can create general pitfalls:

- ❑ The complexity of coordinating a variety of resources is underestimated.
- ❑ Changes to the plan or specification are uncontrolled.
- ❑ Activities are not completed and documented before others begin.
- ❑ The targets of time, cost and quality are unbalanced.

A variety of resources

One of the traits of a project already mentioned is that it requires a variety of resources. This can lead to a number of pitfalls of co-operation during implementation which include:

- ❑ The task of achieving co-operation between unacquainted people is not understood.
- ❑ Different people work by different rules and procedures.
- ❑ The technical methods are too complicated to be fully understood by the users.

Co-operation of unacquainted people

Many people underestimate the difficulty of getting people to work together. This is further complicated if they have not worked together before. In the extreme, no time or effort is put into creating co-operation, because the project manager does not believe it is important.

This may be due to a lack of skill of the project manager, who may not know how to enhance co-operation or who may wrongly believe that the project members are used to working together.

Working by different rules and procedures

Project members may not all work by the same rules and procedures, or work may be documented in different ways. This weakens co-operation and reduces the potential for project members to benefit from each other's experience. It will also reduce the project manager's flexibility, as it will be hard to transfer people from one activity to another. Further, it makes it difficult to introduce new staff, as they must be trained in a variety of procedures. It is vital to define the principles of co-operation, and to establish a common set of rules and procedures to be used by people while working on the project.

Complexity of the technical methods

It is normal for the future users to be represented on the project team. The different experience of the users and the experts can make co-operation difficult. Collaboration can be further complicated by the tools used by the experts. Methods which describe the project's objectives in a way that is foreign to the future users, or use jargon they cannot understand, hamper communication. The experts must describe the project in a language the users can understand, while retaining a degree of precision that describes succinctly the project's intent.

Uncontrolled changes in intent

Changes will inevitably occur during execution of a project, but uncontrolled changes can kill a project, as the members are sucked into the spiral of planning and replanning. Changes must be controlled, and only included in the plan after they have been properly specified.

Starting activities out of turn

If a project team consists of a fixed number of people, members may be under-utilised at times. To stop them becoming dissatisfied, the project manager may find them work by starting work out of sequence, before previous tasks are completed. If the results of the latter turn out to be other than expected, the former must be repeated. All work must be done in the correct order.

Targets of time, cost and quality imbalanced

There are two possible outcomes of this imbalance:

- ❑ Project members seek in vain the perfect solution.
- ❑ Quality control is inadequate.

Seeking perfection

The technical work must not become an objective in its own right. The work is being done to meet the project's goals, which will usually include targets for time and cost. Experts often find it difficult to accept that they are not given the time to find the perfect solution. There is a certain professional prestige in seeking an elegant solution, to which targets of time and cost are secondary. However, sometimes we must accept an imperfect, yet adequate, solution to be on time and to cost. The project manager must exercise the right to choose between perfection and time and cost over-runs. This choice will be made with the end users, who must accept the lower quality, or pay the price.

Inadequate quality control

The choice above was between an imperfect, adequate solution, and targets of time and cost. To be able to judge whether the imperfect solution is adequate, the project manager must plan and control quality so there must be milestones for control throughout the project. Leaving the analysis of quality until the end is dangerous, since it is then impossible to change it without incurring significant cost.

AVOIDING PITFALLS

We have considered a number of pitfalls which we know from experience can cause a project to fail. It is important to dispel any myth that there is some magic formula for estimating or planning a project that guarantees its success. Projects fail for far more fundamental reasons. The list may not be exhaustive, but they must all be avoided if the project is to have the greatest chance of success.

GDPM is a technique that provides methods and tools which help to avoid the pitfalls.

We have also suggested what can be done to avoid these pitfalls. These suggestions are summarised in Figure 3.1 which can be seen as a 'requirement specification' for good project management and good project management tools.

In the following chapters we will describe how project management should be implemented and GDPM will be measured against the requirement specifications, which follow in Figure 3.1.

- The project must work on tasks which are important for the base organisation. There should be a close correlation between the business plans and the objectives of the project

- The base organisation should have principles and policies of project work

- Project methods and tools must compel those involved to spend time on defining project objectives and goals, ie what the project should achieve

- Project methods and tools must compel those involved to focus on giving the project a composite goal, which encompasses matters relating to people, systems (technical matters) and organisation

- Project planning must take place at at least two levels

- Short-term, controllable intermediate goals must be set

- A plan must be clearly presented on a single sheet of standard-sized paper

- Those who draw up the plans must know that they themselves will have to live with the consequences of them

- There must be an understanding of the fact that change processes take time

- There must be an understanding of what control is, and how important this task is in project work

- A plan must be formulated in such a way that it both facilitates and promotes control
- The project manager must be given authority in his dealing with the base organisation
- Procedures for reporting must be established
- There must be an understanding that a project can be organised in several different ways
- The lines of responsibility in the project must be clearly described
- Binding agreements for releasing resources for the project must be drawn up
- Line management and project members should be highly motivated
- A project manager with the right qualities must be selected
- Concrete work must be done to create good conditions for cooperation in the project
- Common methods must be selected for work on the project which also encourage communication between the experts and users
- Changes in project objectives and goals must be made after careful consideration
- There must be quality control throughout the project

Figure 3.1 *Important factors for avoiding pitfalls in projects*

4

Planning Milestones – Focusing on Results

The discussion in the preceding chapter illustrates the importance of planning a project. Without planning you may stumble
into one or more of the pitfalls outlined there. The purpose of
planning is shown in Figure 4.1.

- To achieve a common understanding of the task to be
  resolved
- To obtain an overview of the work to be carried out
- To lay the foundation for allocating and committing
  resources
- To be able to form a suitable organisation of work
- To define a programme of monitoring and control

Figure 4.1 *The purpose of planning*

We differentiate between *milestone planning* and detailed planning (which we also call *activity planning*).

This chapter covers milestone planning, but before we deal
with this we will look at some general aspects of project planning. We will clarify, among other things, the reason for layered
planning.

ASPECTS OF PLANNING

Motivational planning

Planning should provide everyone involved in the project with a
common understanding of the project.

Planning should motivate project members for the task and provide them with a platform for co-operation. The process should stimulate the involvement of interested parties in the planning stages as well as in the subsequent implementation of the plans.

We would go so far as to say that planning should be fun. Planning should be an opportunity to think anew and form different perspectives and to test ideas in a stimulating environment.

We strongly emphasise the motivational and inspirational aspects of planning. They are often neglected in practice so that planning becomes a tedious chore carried out on the project manager's desk or PC. This results in a lack of ownership of the plan by the parties involved in the project and consequently the plan is never actively used. This is one reason for the failure of so many projects.

Planning *must* be a group activity. If all the central project members are involved, they acquire a common insight into the project and a common understanding of future requirements. Our experience is that 80–90 per cent of the time consumed in planning meetings of this kind is devoted to discussions around project content and problem solving. Only 10–20 per cent is formalised planning.

Levels of planning

We divide planning into two fundamentally different levels. This is essential to draw up plans which will be effective in implementation and monitoring as well as getting the involvement of the personnel concerned.

There must be one level where it is decided upon *what* results the project is to deliver, and one level which describes *how* this is going to be achieved. It should be obvious that concentrating on planning *what* should be accomplished before discussing *how* is extremely important. This is called layered planning.

The division into what-planning (goal directed planning) and how-planning (activity planning) does not apply only to the planning of projects. This principle can also be applied in other areas. In marketing, for example, it is natural to discuss what is to be achieved before planning which media should be used and how the advertising campaign should be designed. When designing a computer system, it is necessary to discuss what the computer system should do for the users before discussing how to achieve these goals – if you want useful results.

Planning at these two levels is a prerequisite for success because it means that the planners and all those involved in the project are forced to discuss the challenges of the project in a logical order.

Further, it makes it possible for those interested in the project to become involved in discussions and to obtain information at the level their needs and fields of knowledge dictate. This differentiation of planning levels makes it easier for different categories of interested parties to contribute to the process.

One consequence of a plan should be that interested parties commit themselves to it. Solid commitment is impossible without a good understanding of what the plan involves. It is impossible for those various parties to become involved in a plan and to commit to it if the plan does not concentrate on their specific concerns and areas of responsibility. Therefore, planning in stages is also a prerequisite for establishing commitment in project work.

The most common mistake is that planning is concentrated on the level of detail specifications and crammed with special terminology. The plans do not provide an overview nor do they encourage discussions about the main thrust of the project. The plans only present details. This frightens off the line management and non specialists. They feel that they have nothing to contribute. They lose interest in the project and disclaim responsibility for it.

Such planning makes it impossible to follow up in a meaningful way. Control, ie checking plans against results and taking corrective actions, should also occur at several levels. Levels of planning provide a basis for control at different levels and by different responsible parties; it becomes possible to monitor both the project management and the experts responsible for specific activities in the project.

If the plan has to be revised as a consequence of changes in external conditions or because of internal project matters, it is an advantage if not every change requires the total replanning of the project. When revisions are needed, it is beneficial to have planned the project at different levels.

Global conditions in a project are more stable than the conditions upon which the activities are based. We should have a plan which allows changes at the activity level without having to change the whole plan; changes at the activity level can be introduced without any consequences for the plan at the management level. If there is only one comprehensive plan, there is a great danger that no one will be up to the effort of revising the whole plan when changes in details are made.

On the other hand, if changes are made in the basic conditions for the project, it is important to be able to show clearly how this will affect the plan at the management level. It must be possible to focus on the consequences for the project as a whole. Only then will the top executives and the line management get a clear picture of the changes, and be able to decide on possible measures.

It is obviously essential to have a clear connection between plans at the two levels. It should be comparatively easy to translate the changes at management level into changes at the activity level.

Basis for goal directed management

We have argued above for two levels of planning. The planning at the management level should be concerned with *what* is to be accomplished and not *how* the work shall be done. In other words, this level must be goal-oriented.

In project work, it is quite impractical to operate solely with final goals. It is necessary to have certain checkpoints along the way. We call these checkpoints *milestones*. It should be easy to ascertain whether or not a milestone has been reached. It is not always easy to formulate milestones in this way. But the easier it is to decide whether a milestone has been reached, the easier it becomes to control a project.

The milestones are checkpoints along the way in project work. Thus they have an important function in project management. It is even better if the milestones also provide the company and the line managers with useful results. The milestone then becomes both a checkpoint and a deliverable. We obtain what is called evolutionary development, a gradual fulfilment of project goals. The project does not wait until the last milestone to deliver all the results but aims rather for deliveries in instalments.

Binding plans

The plan at the management level (which we call the milestone plan) shows which end goals and intermediate goals the project should achieve. The plan can be looked upon as a contract between the base organisation and the project. It expresses the commitment undertaken by the project. The commitment rests first and foremost upon the project manager, but no one involved in the project is without responsibility.

This role given to the milestone plan corresponds to how business plans are viewed in other areas of the organisation. A marketing plan is a commitment on the part of the head of marketing and the marketing department to the top executives of the company. It shows what results should be achieved in which markets for which products and to what extent. Like milestone plans, marketing plans do not contain information about activities. Plans for advertisements are not contained in marketing plans, for example, but are included in the internal planning documents in the marketing department.

The milestone plan is a commitment. This does not imply that it cannot be changed, but it means that changes must be made according to an established procedure, involving both the line managers and the project management. To this end, the project should have a responsibility chart showing who must take decisions when the plan is subject to change.

The milestone plan shows the commitment assumed by the project. A prerequisite for this to be met is that the base organisation makes the agreed resources available to the project at the right time. If the base organisation does not fulfil its obligations, the project cannot meet its own.

The commitments must be precisely described in order to avoid misunderstandings or different interpretations. When we liken commitments to contracts this emphasises the importance of having them precisely formulated. The plan must thus show, as clearly as possible, which goals and intermediate goals (milestones) should be achieved. As we will reiterate in the chapter on organisation, the base organisation's commitment to the project must be expressed just as precisely in a responsibility chart.

PRACTICAL MILESTONE PLANNING

Project mandate

In order to make a decision as to whether a project should be started or not, the sponsor needs a description of the important aspects of the project. Various terms are in common use for this, such as project statement, project directive, project outline, etc, but we use the term project mandate.

Figure 4.2 shows what such a description should include.

- The name of the project
- The sponsor or the client of the project
- Background information
- The objectives of the project (the project's contribution to the base organisation)
- The goals of the project
- Limitations on the project
- Budget

Figure 4.2 *The most common elements of the project mandate*

We discuss these elements in more detail below. We show how a project mandate must evolve through analysis and discussion. It is not possible to formulate a good and well thought out project mandate without carrying out basic groundwork.

Many project mandates are set up without the thorough consideration necessary. They must therefore not be regarded as 'sacred cows' which cannot be changed. Through discussions within the project and with the sponsor the project will be described and defined more precisely; it may be expanded, narrowed down, or in certain cases, divided up into several projects.

An oil company in the North Sea set up a project to draw up an inspection system for the platforms and pipelines. When the project began to discuss the inspection task, it was noted quickly that there was a major difference between inspection of the platforms (technical inspection with trained personnel) and inspection of the pipelines (which was to be performed by unmanned submarines). There was no particular purpose to be served in drawing up one common inspection system. As a consequence, there was no reason for establishing a project covering both aspects even if it was in the project mandate.

Objectives and goals

It is useful to start planning by discussing the project's goals. They may be formulated by the project's sponsor and be found in a preliminary project mandate, but there is always a need to elaborate on them and define them more precisely.

A discussion of goals must allow for goals at several levels. Figure 4.3 illustrates different goal concepts.

- The objectives of the base organisation
- The objectives of the project (the purpose of the project; its contribution to the base organisation)
- The goals of the project
  - Main goals
  - Result goals (main goals divided into more detailed and measurable goals)

Figure 4.3 *Different goal concepts*

When determining project goals you must, at least with regard to PSO projects, anchor your discussions in the organisation which the project is intended to change and improve.

Every business is established to fulfil certain objectives. A college is set up to educate; a consulting firm offers advisory services; a factory manufactures and sells a certain product. In addition to carrying out the tasks for which it is intended, a business must have managing functions and administrative support functions (accounting, personnel administration and payroll departments, for example).

The legitimacy of the project lies in the fact that, in one way or another, it will enable the organisation to achieve better its main objectives or improve its performance of the managing or supporting functions. In order to pinpoint what the project will do for the business, it is often useful to describe the organisation's main objectives and managing and supporting functions. This is done using what we call the *objective breakdown structure*. This method of defining the project's tasks more precisely is presented in Chapter 10. It is important to look at the project from such a perspective. Individual projects tend to have a life of their own after a certain period of time, without considering that they exist to satisfy an objective or needs in the organisation.

For the time being we will content ourselves with emphasising that a project should always fulfil or support organisational objectives or needs. When public projects are concerned it is often necessary to regard the whole of society as the base organisation. The project should thus contribute to realising a society's objectives or needs.

A project cannot work for every objective or every managing or supporting function in a business; decisions must be made about which elements the project should promote. The objectives of the project are thus to contribute to the organisation's ability to perform some of its tasks in some new or improved way.

A car importer wanted to develop a computer-based customer service system, a common project task. Before taking on the task, discussions were held about what the company wished to achieve. It emerged from these discussions that it was looking for a better way to treat customers which would encourage them to remain customers for life. This insight lead to an analysis of which aspects of car ownership and maintenance gave rise to brand loyalty and what *that* implied for service and quality standards in all branches of the company. Only after this process was the objective of the project clarified. The project thus developed from the simple development of a computer system to a composite project where staff also worked to improve service and quality in all customer contact. The project had acquired an objective which genuinely supported something of importance for the company.

In another example, a company determined that it wanted an improved financial management information system. However, again we emphasise that it is important not to take this requirement immediately at face value, but to consider the business need which the project should address. In this case, the underlying need was to manage better the acquisition and utilisation of resources, both people and equipment. That was the area in which the project had to make a contribution. For this purpose a computer system was required which had to fulfil certain technical and functional requirements. Equally important, however, were organisational development and professional development of the employees which would lead to a better use of resources within the company.

Product development is another common project task. The starting point must be to determine what the business expects of a new product. It must satisfy certain customer needs and at the same time meet requirements, for example, for cost effectiveness and the ability to fit into the existing production and market profile. Even such an innovative project does not lead a life independent of the organisation. On the contrary, it must develop its ideas in harmony with the base organisation and its objectives.

The project's objective (or purpose) makes clear what kind of contribution the project will make for the business. The goals of the project state more concretely what it will deliver to the base organisation.

The project goals form a hierarchy, where the goals on a lower level define more precisely and elaborate on the goals of the level above. The need for details depends on the size of the project.

The main goals of the project show which areas are the main areas of business to be addressed. A thorough discussion of what the organisation wants usually provides a good basis for establishing these goals.

In each case, a PSO test of the main goals should be carried out. This means that several goal-related questions should be answered. First, is there a goal for developing the people concerned? Second, is there a goal which states which 'technical items' will be produced by the project? Third, is there a goal for developing the organisation or its environment?

A municipality proposed a project which would improve public transportation in the region. The project's objective was improved public transportation in region X. Two main goals were formulated. One was that the trains should run more frequently. The second was that the bus service should be expanded.

A PSO test of these main goals showed that they were purely 'technical'. Shouldn't the project also have 'P' and 'O' goals? Further discussion led to two additional main goals. One was that there should be an improvement in regional cooperation between municipal agencies and the transportation providers (in other words an organisational goal). The second was that the citizens' attitude toward public transportation had to change. People had to look less favourably on private transportation and more positively on public transportation (in other words a people development goal).

Segmentation

Before starting a project it is wise to assess whether it is beneficial to divide the project into parts. There are several reasons for segmentation being advantageous. Figure 4.4 shows the most important grounds.

Decisions concerning the division of a project should be deferred until after the project's objective has been established.

- The project is large
- The project is long-term
- It is advantageous to have several parallel sub-projects subordinate to a main project
- We do not have the information to plan the whole project as one unit
- The project has several natural phases with completely different contents

Figure 4.4 *Some important reasons for segmenting a project*

Division must be determined in each individual case. What is considered a reasonable division will be strongly influenced by what the project is intended to do.

It is often expedient to divide a project to achieve a more manageable situation. A project which is large in terms of scope and duration might profit both administratively and managerially from being divided into several smaller projects. These advantages must be balanced against the disadvantage of being unable to manage all aspects of the task in one project.

A project may be maintained as a single unit, but be divided up into several sub-projects. Each sub-project will be a part of the main project. This simplifies administrative matters while at the same time the common connection to the main project allows the different tasks to be seen in relationship to each other. Sub-projects may be run consecutively or simultaneously.

A completely different reason for dividing a project is that it may not be possible to plan the whole project as one unit. The task may be such that information gathered and decisions taken at a certain stage of the project determine which activities should be carried out later in the project. As the result of the decisions are not yet known, there is no purpose to be served in drawing up a single plan. The last section of the plan will only consist of generalities because at the time the plan is made there is no clarity about what should be done at the later stages of the project.

Often people draw up poor plans because they feel compelled to plan the whole project as one unit. They lack information and the plan is thus a poor one to which it is impossible to adhere. The project will then be considered unsuccessful.

Dividing the project into a feasibility phase (which may be called a preliminary project or feasibility study) and an implementation phase (or main project) is one way of tackling this problem. In the feasibility study we describe problems more precisely, determine the objectives and goals of the project and take decisions on how to approach the problems. In the main project we implement what has been decided. In the next section we will examine more closely the distinction between these two kinds of projects.

The world, however, is not always so straightforward that it allows us to get all the problem defining and solving out of the way first and then carry on with the implementation. In practice, problem resolution occurs on several levels, where we have both problem defining activities and implementation activities. Therefore, even in the main project there may be a need to analyse, evaluate and make decisions.

It is therefore appropriate to consider whether the project ought to be divided up into several smaller parts, which we call phases. This is relevant both in feasibility projects and implementation projects. A characteristic of a phase is that it is possible to plan it as a whole. This means that planning can give us an insight into the types of activities that should be done in this phase.

A product development project can naturally be divided into a number of different phases. There may be one phase for design and engineering, one phase for preparing the new product for production, one phase where the product is introduced into the general production system and a marketing phase. Some of these phases follow each other chronologically. It is not possible to prepare the product for production before completing the design and construction phase. On the other hand, it is not necessary to wait until the product is in production before starting the marketing phase. Planning for marketing can be initiated once the central decisions on design and engineering have been made. In this way market momentum is not lost.

Another project was to improve the quality of the daily operations of the base organisation and also lead to ISO certification. The project started with a mapping and consciousness-raising phase, after which followed several parallel phases to improve quality in different areas.

A research programme to acquire information on how to reduce pollution from livestock manure started with a traditional feasibility study (to discover what should be researched). After that five parallel sub-projects were started, scheduled to last for a four-year period and to be concluded with scientific reports. Two years before the scientific work is scheduled to be completed, a sub-project will be started with the task of collating the information acquired thus far and developing recommendations on how farmers could reduce pollution. It was decided to release research results before all the scientific work had been completed, because it was expected that there would be useful results to pass on to the agricultural industry.

When a project is divided into phases or sub-projects, it is necessary to discuss what goal each individual phase or sub-project is expected to achieve.

Feasibility study and main project

A feasibility study has different tasks from those of a main project. It should define precisely the objectives and goals of the project. It should work out which types of solutions can be used to achieve the goals, evaluate them and make further recommendations for a main project. The recommendations should be accompanied by financial plans and progress plans.

In the main project, whatever tasks have been decided upon in the feasibility study are accomplished.

In general, too little weight is given to the feasibility study. This applies to all types of projects, and has serious consequences.

The starting point for the feasibility study is usually the project mandate. This outlines the problems or opportunities which form the background for starting the project. The goals for the project are formulated, but, as indicated previously, they can be fairly imprecise. Ideas on solutions to the problems or opportunities may also be found in the written material or verbal instructions which initiate the project.

The feasibility study works further on formulating the goals. Imprecise and vague goals make later work in the project difficult and may cause project members to pull in different directions because they have different understandings of what the project is trying to achieve. Poorly formulated goals also greatly reduce the likelihood of a successful outcome.

A central task of a feasibility study is to identify possible alternatives, the different types of solutions that one has to choose from. If a feasibility study is not carried out, or if the work is superficial, this may mean that one alternative (a certain solution) is selected without thorough analysis and evaluation. This is one of the main reasons that a project does not provide the base organisation with the results it expects.

In a project intended to propose a computer solution for an administrative problem, it is crucially important that the feasibility study succeeds in finding and evaluating different types of solutions. Should the project develop the needed software itself? Should they buy a standard software package which can be installed without any alterations? Should they buy and then modify a standard software package?

Creativity is important in a feasibility study. If people are inventive in finding different possible solutions, it provides a good starting point for selecting the correct solution.

A feasibility study must evidently address the question of feasibility. The different possible solutions should thus be identified and the suitability of the alternatives should be evaluated, as to their organisational, financial and technical feasibility. An assessment should be made to determine which alternative has the best chance of reaching the stated goals.

It can be seen from the above that there are two separate tasks which are dealt with in a feasibility study. The first is work on defining precisely what the project should achieve. The second is an identification, evaluation and selection of alternative solutions. These two tasks may be represented as two phases in the feasibility study.

In the example regarding the purchase of a computer system, the development of a requirement specification (which shows what the computer solution should do for the company) is the first phase, while selection of the particular computer solution constitutes the second phase.

A main project (which is also called an implementation project) differs in character from a feasibility study. Creativity and analytical work are not at the forefront of a main project, but rather thoroughness, completeness and systematic work. It is important that all aspects of implementation are covered by the plans.

The feasibility study and the main project are planned separately. It is not realistic to plan the main project before the feasibility study has been completed. Planning of the main project may possibly be the final part of the feasibility study, in which case the mandate for the feasibility project would make it clear this is included in its scope.

Name

Choosing the right name for the project is important. It might seem strange that the designation of a project is significant, but a name sends strong signals about what a project is about. The attitude of both the line management and the project team is affected by the name.

Whether we like it or not, a project's name says something about the project. It is important that the project's name provides all the right associations and an understanding of what the project is aiming to achieve. It is often appropriate that the objective of the project be reflected in its name. The objective expresses what the project should achieve, but the name should perhaps in a few words present a 'sales pitch' so that people immediately have a picture of what the project is aiming at. If a phase (sub-project) in a larger project is given its own name, the name should reflect the objective of that part of the project.

Some examples illustrate the importance of a good project name. A project in an insurance company was first described as 'Finance Section Reorganisation'. It was decided instead to call it 'Reorganising the finance section for better customer service'.

The first name is associated with pure reorganisation, to which many will immediately have a negative reaction. The second clarifies the purpose of the reorganisation and creates motivation for the project.

A retail chain established a project to develop a lighting system for its stores. The project was to find and purchase light fittings for the stores. The first proposal for a name, naturally enough, was 'Store Lighting System'. It would have been easy to believe that this was a purely technical project. A name which better illustrated what was to be achieved, however, was 'Sales Display Lighting for Retail Stores'. Thus everyone involved understood that this was a project which also affected the stores' income. Interest in the project and commitment to it then changed significantly.

The development of a departmental report to be presented to Parliament can be regarded as a project which involves many people, both inside and outside the department. One such project was first labelled 'Development of a departmental report on the reorganisation of the central administration of education'. This designation gave the impression of a purely specialist task; some departmental bureaucrats were to write a report for Parliament. The name was changed to 'Political support for a departmental report on . . .'. The task was no different from the previous one; all departmental reports must have political support. This new name, however, painted a clearer picture of the project. Everyone understood that a report was to be written, but now the name highlighted the fact that this report must have support among the department's political leaders as well as of other politicians. It called attention to the fact that political aspects must be worked on in parallel with the formulation of the contents of the report.

The project 'To establish the State Film Institute' was renamed 'To establish and develop the State Film Institute for effective encouragement and promulgation of Norwegian films and film culture'. The name then illustrated the purpose of establishing the new institute.

Project names have had a tendency to be a bit long and detailed. A short, explicit name is better than a long one.

Many projects also acquire so-called acronyms, a word formed from the first letters of a complete name. PSO is an acronym for people, system and organisation development. It is by far the best when an acronym for a project expresses the same concept as is contained in the complete project name, or the project's objective.

Milestones and milestone planning

Let us now suppose that we have progressed to the point in the project where we have described the project's objective and its various goals. We have also divided it into parts, for example into certain phases or sub-projects. We are now tackling the first phase (or sub-project) in the project. We are discussing which goals this phase should realise, and after this we can start work on drawing up a plan for this phase of the project.

The plan will consist of several milestones and show the dependencies between them. We call the plan a milestone plan.

Milestones are checkpoints in the project which enable us to ensure that we are on the right track. A milestone is a description of the state the project should be in at a certain stage.

A milestone describes what the project should achieve, not how. As far as possible a milestone should be neutrally formulated with regard to the solution.

We said that a milestone is a description of the state of the project at a certain stage. The word 'state' can be explained by giving some examples of 'everyday' states:

❑ Being awake at 06:30.
❑ Being at work 'on time'.
❑ Having achieved a planned result at work.
❑ Being full.

Such states can be described without indicating which activities have been performed to achieve them. We understand immediately that the state of being 'awake at 06:30' can be achieved with the help of several different types of activity, for example:

❑ You can go to bed early in order to wake up on your own.
❑ You can be awakened by an alarm clock.

❏ You can be woken up by another person.

Similarly, the state of being 'full' can be achieved by going to a restaurant and eating, or by other activities such as shopping for food yourself, preparing the food and then eating it.

Most people, including project members, are not accustomed to thinking in terms of states. People are usually most concerned with activities. Therefore, awareness is required when formulating milestones so that there is a real focus on states which are neutral with regard to the solution.

There is a great difference in saying that a milestone has been reached 'when the members have specified knowledge in a stated area' and saying that the milestone has been reached 'when the members have completed course X'. In the latter instance we do not have a formula which is neutral with regard to the solution. Instead we have an activity-orientated formula. We have, at an early planning stage, tied ourselves to a specific activity (course X) instead of having the freedom at a later stage to choose the activities which will provide the members with the desired background. Neither does the latter formula allow quality control in the same way as a description of state. A project member may not necessarily have acquired particular knowledge even if the person concerned has participated in the course.

We will return to the formulation of milestones, but first let us set up an example of milestone planning. The interpretation of such a plan is important. (In project literature there are several 'network plans', all having their own particular interpretation. It should not be assumed that because you have seen one kind of plan you know how to interpret them all.)

The milestone plan in Figure 4.5 should be understood as follows. In order to reach milestone M5 we must have been in the state described by milestone M4. Similarly, we cannot reach M4 before realising M3, and so on.

A milestone plan is a logical plan. It shows the logical dependencies relevant to the current project work.

In order to reach a specific milestone, a series of activities must have been completed. Some people believe that the milestone plan shows that the work involved in reaching one milestone cannot be started before the previous milestone has been

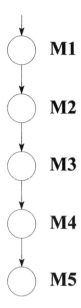

Figure 4.5 *Milestone plan*

reached. This is incorrect, and may be the result of conflicting interpretations from other types of network planning. In general, you do not need to wait until the previous milestone has been reached before starting to work on another. Figure 4.6 illustrates the relationship between activities and milestones.

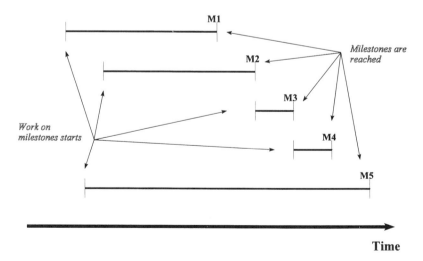

Figure 4.6 *Correlation between activities and milestones*

It may sometimes be the case that work on the next milestone cannot begin before the previous one has been reached. (The figure shows that work on M3 starts when M2 is reached and work on M4 starts when M3 is reached in this instance.)

Work on a milestone may build directly upon the result achieved by the previous milestone, but most often it is either necessary or expedient to start working earlier on a milestone. Work on a specific milestone can commence while work on the previous one is in progress. (The figure illustrates this for milestone M2; work on it has started before M1 has been reached.) It may also be the case that work on a later milestone in the project starts before starting work on the preceding milestone in the series. (The figure shows that work towards M5 has started before work towards M3 and M4 has started.)

While work on the various milestones can begin out of sequence, it is important to keep the essence of the milestone plan in mind; a milestone cannot be reached (work towards reaching this milestone cannot be completed) before the previous milestone has been reached.

Let us look at an example of a milestone plan. In order to make this as simple as possible we will not look at a PSO project but consider a specialist project. The managing director in a company has given a group of experts the task of drawing up an action plan to determine how to improve the work environment within the company. A milestone plan for this project is shown in Figure 4.7.

The milestone plan shows that a description of the present situation should be developed first. It is important to note that the milestone plan does not say anything about how this should be done. For example, all employees or only a group of employees may be interviewed or sent questionnaires. No decision is taken at this stage on how the milestone is to be reached. First, what the project is to achieve should be determined; then a discussion on how to achieve it can take place. Note that such a description of the present situation can be valuable in itself. It is advantageous to have a picture of the actual work environment. The milestone does not only serve as a checkpoint in the work

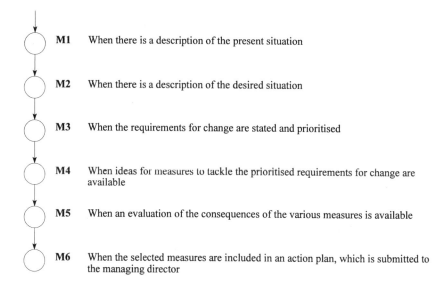

M1	When there is a description of the present situation	
M2	When there is a description of the desired situation	
M3	When the requirements for change are stated and prioritised	
M4	When ideas for measures to tackle the prioritised requirements for change are available	
M5	When an evaluation of the consequences of the various measures is available	
M6	When the selected measures are included in an action plan, which is submitted to the managing director	

Figure 4.7 *Milestone plan for a project which will draw up an action plan to improve the work environment*

towards a completed project; it can also provide valuable information for the business.

The next milestone requires a description of the desired situation. Work on developing a picture of the desired work environment may start before a description of the present situation exists. It may, for example, be relevant to interview line managers and trade union representatives. A final description of the desired situation is not possible, however, before the description of the present situation has been completed; the description of the desired situation must take into account all the conditions mentioned in the description of the present situation.

The requirements for change will be the difference between the desired situation and the present situation. It is self-evident that it is impossible to obtain an overview of all the requirements for change and to prioritise them for action before obtaining the description of the desired situation. Ideas for measures to be taken must be generated, but at this stage we do not take any decisions on how to arrive at them. The consequences of the various measures must be evaluated and the best measures will be included in an action plan.

So much for the example. It underlines the central point that the milestone plan is set up without taking any decisions on which activities must be started to reach the different milestones. This means that a milestone plan can be read and understood without having detailed insight into the underlying activities. For this reason also we call it a *logical* plan; it shows the logical dependencies between the states.

Experience shows that the milestone plan functions as an effective means of communication between the base organisation and the project. It is important in this regard that the line management feel they have a plan to which they can relate. It shows, in a lucid manner, what the project is to achieve and the relationships between the different project milestones. We have also experienced that any omissions and logical flaws in the milestone plan will be discovered by the line management and line members. This is a good indication that people understand the plan and its implications. It is also of importance that when the plan is accepted and understood by the line management, they too can use it as a means of control.

We have emphasised the significance of having a plan at the management level which does not have to be reassessed if changes occur at the activity level. Naturally, there is a particular need for this type of plan when working in unfamiliar areas, where the necessary activities are not known in detail. The milestone plan remains in force, even if it is decided to work forwards to a specific milestone by methods other than those originally considered.

It is psychologically important for monitoring purposes to have a plan whose contents and appearance do not change for each reporting period. Frequent changes of a plan easily lead to monitoring being taken less seriously.

As a rule a milestone plan is easy to read and understand. This does not imply that it is easy to draw it up. Significant intellectual effort may be required to formulate a good milestone plan. We have already described it as a logical plan. This is because the making of a plan requires logical consideration of the states a project must pass through to achieve its goals.

We have now presented the central concepts of the milestone plan. A good milestone plan requires well-formulated milestones. We will therefore examine in more detail what requirements we expect a well-formulated milestone to meet. Figure 4.8 summarises the important factors.

- A milestone text may often comprise two elements:
  * the state to be achieved
  * conditions necessary to achieve the state
- A milestone should be controllable
- Important decision-making points in the project should be milestones

---

Figure 4.8 *Some important 'requirements' for milestones*

It is desirable that milestones should be seen to be natural by those who read and use the milestone plan. What is considered natural obviously depends on the experience and knowledge in the area of work within which the project falls. Decisions traditionally regarded as being important in the current type of project are an example of natural milestones.

It is important that a milestone is described in such a way that it is possible to ascertain that the desired state has been reached. This is the crux of this method of project management. It is impossible to have goal directed project management if it is not possible to check that an actual state has been reached.

It is easiest to confirm that a milestone has been reached when it concerns something visible that can be physically inspected. It is considerably more difficult with qualitative conditions: When has a manager become a better manager? How can we confirm that the environment has improved? It is possible to work on such qualitative conditions *ad infinitum*. It is therefore important to formulate the milestone in such a way that it describes some form of end point; it must indicate when the work can be considered completed and the result good enough.

In this context it is significant to note that the formulation of a milestone may comprise two elements, both a description of the desired situation (which we have stressed up to this point) and a description of the conditions attached to achieving this state. The conditions provide a precise expression of what must be done to ensure quality. In cases where it is not easy to quality control the desired state, it is all the more important to indicate what must be done before we can say that the desired state has been achieved.

The conditions provide the requirements for the desired quality of a milestone. A condition may refer to:

❑ Methods which allow the result to be quality controlled.
❑ Procedures (the intention is that the use of a specific procedure will ensure quality).
❑ Previous work.
❑ What professional approval should be obtained (the intention is then that quality will be ensured by having a qualified person or qualified body approve the milestone).

Even if we use conditional elements in the milestone formulation, we try to adhere to the requirement of neutrality regarding the solution. Conditions should not suggest a detailed solution, but simply express which requirements must be met.

We will give some examples of milestone formulations. The sections referring to states in the milestones are in italics:

❑ *Suppliers are selected* on the basis of an approved purchasing procedure.
❑ *A proposal* exists and is *approved by the managing director* after a thorough review.
❑ *The description of administrative routines is available, described* with the help of PSO graphs.
❑ *Requirements for expertise and skills are met* after an approved training programme has been held.
❑ *Users have proved that they can manage independently* after the agreed training programme has been held.

The conditional element indicates the type of activities which must be carried out or tools which must be used. We use this to ensure quality in a milestone which is otherwise difficult to check for quality. However, the conditional element also makes it possible to limit the number of milestones and still make sure that the activities to ensure quality take place.

The second milestone formulation listed above could have been divided into two parts: firstly, one that requires that the results of the review be documented, followed by another that requires that the proposal be approved by the boss. In the last two formulations we could have the completion of the training programme as a separate milestone.

A milestone plan should provide an overview of the whole project. In order to obtain this, there should not be too many milestones. How many is a matter of judgement, but we believe that there should be fewer than 20. The maximum lies, perhaps, around 15. Use of milestones which are descriptions of states containing one or more conditions reduces the need for the number of milestones in a quality-oriented plan.

Several more examples of formulations taken from actual plans follow:

❏ *Measures to promote employment are prioritised* based on the city's financial resources and the effects on unemployment.
❏ *An objective breakdown structure is available* and so precise that the structure provides all members with a common understanding of the service objectives, enabling them to determine result goals.
❏ *A description of managerial roles and responsibilities within the organisation exists* after all managers have drawn up their own descriptions based on a background of completed training and awareness-raising programmes.
❏ *A plan for a further improvement in results exists* after an evaluation has been made.
❏ *A new product is available to the users.*

Result paths

Until now we have shown a milestone plan where each milestone is only dependent on one other. This is a rather one-dimensional plan, and not particularly typical of project work. A project usually covers several needs or objectives in a business; it usually has a composite goal, and the plan is therefore multi-dimensional. This means that several aspects of the project are worked on simultaneously.

In order to bring out the multi-dimensional aspects of project work, we introduce what we call a result path. A result path is a series of milestones which are especially closely connected to each other. A result path is formed by milestones which all contribute to the creation of a certain result. The links between the result paths show that work on the different types of results is interdependent. Figure 4.9 shows a milestone plan with result paths.

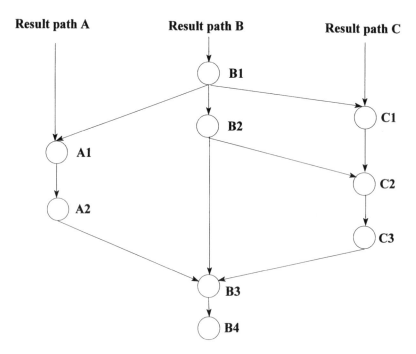

Figure 4.9 *Milestone plan with result paths*

In this case the plan has three result paths. The number of paths in a plan depends on the nature of the project, specifically, on how many major results will be created. We can thus have a plan with only one path. A plan with two to four paths is most usual.

With five paths we probably will have a plan which is too complex.

Each path is given a name which describes what is going on in that part of the project. The first one or two letters in the designation may be included in a reference code to identify the milestones. In the figure the three result paths are called A, B and C. The milestones in path A are assigned the labels A1 and A2, the milestones in path B are called B1, B2, B3 and B4, and so on.

We can see from the milestone plan that milestone A2 cannot be reached before A1 has been reached. As we saw in the simplest plans, there is a dependent relationship between milestones in an individual result path. We can also see, however, that neither A1 nor C1 can be reached before B1 has been realised. B3 requires that both B2 and C3 are reached. Thus the plan also shows that there are dependencies between the paths. Work on one project result depends on what has been achieved in other areas.

Milestone B4 is the end milestone in this project. It has an important position in a project, but realisation of the project goals should not rest on this milestone alone. It is a positive and useful factor if some goals have already been realised via previous milestones. For example, it may be that the achievement of A2 means that the goals linked to the part of the project covered by result path A have been reached. C3 may play a corresponding role for result path C. And it may even be that certain goals have already been achieved at earlier project milestones. In any case, realisation of B4 means that all the project goals have been achieved, giving the final milestone a special significance.

It may be a difficult task to find good result paths, but this is an important aspect of planning because the result paths signal to the reader what results the project is aiming to achieve.

Earlier we discussed the importance of dividing a project into phases. When we are faced with the task of drawing up a milestone plan, we have already divided the project into phases and we are subsequently going to draw up a milestone plan for a certain phase of the project. Furthermore, we should have formulated goals for this phase (which are not the same as the goals for the whole project).

Goals for the phase can be used as a starting point for a result path in the milestone plan. A goal expresses precisely the fact that we want to achieve a specific type of result. Therefore, goals are suitable as the basis for divisions into result paths. If three goals have been set for the phase in question, they often provide a point of departure for three different result paths in the plan.

Before making a final decision on the result paths, other matters should be taken into consideration. It should be determined whether any specific problems should be focused on, or whether there are any conditions especially critical for the success of the endeavour. For example, we might consider quality assurance to be a critical factor for success. In that case, quality assurance could become a separate result path. We might also regard building support for the project in the base organisation to be of vital importance for its success. This could be a separate result path. In general, however, it is best to use the goals as the bases for setting up result paths. Attention should then be paid to such matters as quality and support in connection with each individual milestone in the various phases.

Result paths vary from phase to phase in a project. The reason for this, of course, is that the results we create in one phase will be essentially different from those created in another phase. There are, for example, always different result paths for a feasibility study and for a main project.

In our first example of a milestone plan (Figure 4.7) we had only one result path. The project task was to draw up an action plan to improve the work environment in a business. The task can be expanded to drawing up a plan to improve both the physical and social work environment. With the goal formulated like this it is natural to have one result path for the physical environment and one for the social environment. Work on the plan will certainly reveal that there are dependencies between these two paths.

We have a further expansion of the task if the managing director states that the project, in addition to developing an action plan, should also create an increased awareness of the importance of an improved work environment in the company. There will then be a need for a result path for raising awareness in addition to the two already identified. It also changes the character of the project from being a specialist project to becoming a PSO project.

This brief example illustrates how the use of result paths clarifies the project itself. It provides a plan which the proposer of the project and the base organisation can relate to because it shows that the project is working on tasks which the organisation wants to solve.

We will give several more examples of result-path thinking in projects.

A light fitting factory wanted to develop a range of fittings which would be better designed and more functional than earlier products. At the same time the products would have to be profitable. In the milestone plan there was one result path for the design, another for functionality and a third for profitability. It is self-evident that after the first phase is completed and the design and functionality have been worked out, these elements will not be relevant result paths in further work.

A company wanted to install a new local area network for its data processing. In the project set up, the first phase was to select a network. The purpose of the network was to cover the users' requirements for data processing services. It had to be cost effective and, in addition, it had to meet requirements for security and accessibility. Four result paths were selected: user requirements, network, finance and security/accessibility. The result paths immediately showed what was important for the project when choosing a network.

Another company wanted a computer-based standard package for finance functions. The task was very similar to the project for selecting a network. In the feasibility study the result paths in this case were:

- ❑ Organisation and work processes.
- ❑ Functional needs and requirements.
- ❑ Technological and operational needs and requirements.
- ❑ Choice of a standard package and need for modifications.

The implementation phase had completely different result paths. Here, they could use the PSO philosophy with one path for development of people (training and motivation), one for modification, implementation, and testing, and one for organisational development with the introduction of new routines and patterns of responsibilities.

A municipality wanted to draw up an overall plan to prioritise and organise employment measures for their unemployed. The result paths were characterised by the considerations in a good plan. They set up result paths to:

❑ Categorise and prioritise the unemployed.
❑ Identify and select measures.
❑ Assess costs and benefits and ensure that the plan is financially feasible.
❑ Identify departments, companies and voluntary organisations which could contribute to the measures and enter into agreements with them.

Forming the milestone plan

The following is advice on how to do milestone planning in practise. We emphasise that milestone planning is group work. It is important that a sense of community develops around the plan. It is also important that the various types of expertise required for the project be utilised.

For group work to function well, physical conditions must be favourable. Everyone must have a fair opportunity to participate actively. One possibility is to use a flip chart. Everyone can see what is written on the large sheets of paper and it is easy to use different colours. A further point is that the sheets can be torn off when they are covered with text and symbols, and hung up around the room. The sheets should 'decorate' the room so that it is easy to keep a continuous overview of all the ideas contributed by the participants.

Another possibility is that everyone write down a proposal for milestones on 'post-it' slips (slips with an adhesive strip on the reverse side, so that they can be positioned and then moved about later on). This allows the participants to discuss the dependencies between different milestones and their positions in a result path and illustrate the points by moving the slips on which the milestones are noted.

At the end of the planning session the milestone plan should be converted into a finished outline. This should also be done by the group. It is damaging to the spirit of cooperation if one person sits by himself in a corner and draws up a proposal. Everyone should participate in this phase too.

In order to get the whole group involved in the conversion to a finished outline, we recommend the use of an overhead projector and a white-board. We place a milestone form on the projector. This will then be projected on the white-board, and one person draws up the milestone plan while everyone joins in and makes comments. The point of using the white-board is that it is then very easy to alter the milestone plan allowing for each proposal contributed by the participants. A flip chart is not suitable in this phase. When everyone is agreed on what the plan should look like, it can be drawn up on a milestone form. This is simply a matter of copying.

We recommend that the group start by discussing the goals for the current phase and agree on a rough draft of the goals before proceeding any further. The goals can be revised later, but there should be a rough draft.

After this you can discuss result paths. This is an essential step in the process. It is no exaggeration to say that the difference between good and poor milestone plans often lies in managing to find good result paths, as we have already illustrated.

It is important also to find appropriate designations for the paths. Experience has shown that good names contribute to raising the quality of the milestone plan.

When a proposal for paths is accepted, you can begin to look for milestones. You may work on each path separately. It is wise to describe the end milestone first and then any other milestones which are part of the end result. It is important that everyone has the same understanding of what the project intends to achieve. We recommend, however, that you do not spend too much time on the end milestone because it can be expected to take a different shape later on when the group has acquired better insight into and understanding of the project. Indeed, the project's various goals can be achieved in several ways and are not connected solely to the end milestone.

You can then seek out relevant milestones more freely. The group needs to do a great deal of work on formulating each milestone. It is easy to underestimate the value of this work, but it is important so that each member gains an understanding both of the project work to be carried out and of the task of controlling the project.

During the discussion of milestones, proposals for activities will arise. The discussion should not concern itself with activities, but it is important that the activities mentioned are noted so that they can be discussed later on. If we start discussions on activities at this stage, the milestone plan will often become activity-orientated, and not state-orientated, as we wish it to be. Nevertheless, certain activities can provide ideas for milestones, and it is therefore undesirable to have a total ban on the mention of activities.

Evaluation

When a draft for a milestone plan has been developed, it is necessary to carry out a comprehensive evaluation of it.

Firstly, is the scope of the plan balanced? It should have approximately the same degree of detail throughout. Some parts should not be significantly more detailed than others. If the first part of the project is planned in great detail while the final part is so rough and diffuse that you can hardly work out what the milestones represent, it implies that the planning horizon was too distant.

This raises the question of how far forward you should plan. In general we say that you should not plan any further forward than is practical, but what is practical varies from project to project. In many projects, decisions are made during the initial planning stage that determine the direction of the project and the activities that will actually be carried out in the final stages. It is not particularly practical to plan the whole project at once, when at the time of planning you do not know what the latter sections of the project will deal with and what types of activity will then be relevant. It is inappropriate, and a way of deceiving yourself and others, to draw up a plan where the final stages consist solely of generalities because you do not know what tasks will be involved.

This is an unfamiliar concept for many project managers. They realize that it is practical to divide a project into a feasibility study and a main project. Many, however, do not realise that it may also be necessary to divide the project further into phases in order to be able to draw up meaningful plans.

A PSO project is characterised by the fact that the choice of the project's direction and approach should depend on a maturation process in the earliest stages of the project involving learning and the development of attitudes. In such cases it is inappropriate to start the project by establishing what should occur later on. Drawing up one plan for the whole project is not recommended.

In projects where a proposal is to be submitted in reply to an invitation to tender, the situation forces you to plan the whole project as one unit. In such cases requirements must be set at the outset for what will actually be executed in the later phases. In purely technical projects, where you have a good idea about most of the actual project activities, this may not cause difficulties. In a PSO project this type of overall plan can prove to be a considerable hindrance to rational work later in the project. When the plan begins to appear inadequate, you may decide to stick to it and make silly mistakes. Or you can deviate from the plan, choose a new direction which you now understand to be best, but be criticised because the plan was not good enough.

We have already stressed several times the importance of good result paths. They should reflect the goals of the project and show the areas within which the results are to be achieved. People in the base organisation should be able to understand immediately what is represented by each individual path.

In principle you should have the benefit of all the result paths throughout the entire milestone plan. You should not find that you finish a result path early in the milestone plan. This indicates either an incorrect choice of result path or missing milestones.

The plan's logical construction must be checked by others than those who drew it up. Detailed knowledge of project activities should be unnecessary for participating in a review of the plan. The milestone plan should be easily understood by everyone who needs to be involved in it. Top management and line management cannot accept a plan that they cannot understand.

The milestone formulations must also be checked, according to the requirements which we set earlier for a milestone.

The milestone plan only stipulates that one milestone must be reached before the subsequent one can be reached. It does not say anything about when work towards achieving a milestone can begin. In order to obtain this kind of information you have to look at the responsibility chart, which we will discuss later.

A milestone plan should be contained on one page. This is important for helping everyone get an overview and understand the plan. Plans that take even two pages, for example, are not as easy to comprehend.

Every once in a while, we hear the assertion that 'it is not possible to draw up a one-page plan for our project'. We have yet to find an instance where this is true. It is always possible to draw up a rational and serviceable milestone plan on one page.

In some cases milestones have to be combined. We do have an upper limit for the number of milestones that there can be in one plan. This might cause worry that the plan will not then include all the states the project must logically go through. However, we can link several conditions to the milestones selected, and thus cover what must be done before each milestone is reached.

The milestone plan will naturally be supplemented with more detailed plans and we will go into this later.

EXAMPLE OF MILESTONE PLANNING AND MILESTONE PLANS

We will illustrate the GDPM method with a comprehensive example. We have chosen to construct an example rather than use an actual case in order to be able to present as many points as possible in an easily comprehensible manner.

We will look at a company which is a market leader within a sector of the electronic and computer field. It has approximately 200 employees. The company sells its products both to private individuals and businesses. It provides training and offers maintenance for the products.

At the outset it is located at three sites in Oslo. It provides poor customer service and is operated inefficiently.

At the beginning of December a project manager was appointed and assigned the task of managing the move to new premises. This was to occur before the end of the following year, as the lease agreements for the present three locations expired then.

Management also decided that the company should use the relocation and integration of operations to raise the total quality of the company's work. The project was given a free hand with regard to renting or buying the new premises, although the majority believed that purchase was more appropriate.

The project's objective and goals

The project's objective expresses why the project has been established. It demonstrates what the project should achieve for the business, in this case our example company.

The project should contribute to improved customer service and a more efficient operation. These are the main elements in the project's objective. This may seem to be somewhat vague, so part of the project will involve clarifying the project's objective. In Chapter 10 we examine how this is done in more detail.

The project's objective (or vision) is thus 'Improved customer service and more efficient operations in new premises'. A project's goals express how the project can contribute to fulfilling the objectives of the business. In this case the main project goals are that the company establish itself under one roof, improve customer service, and develop more efficient operations.

Division into phases or sub-projects

This project has two clear phases:

- ❑ Work leading to the signing of the lease or purchase contract.
- ❑ Work from the time the premises have been selected until relocation is completed.

The first phase is mainly in the nature of a feasibility study; in the second phase the emphasis is on implementation. It is easy to understand that it is not particularly practical to plan the move before knowing the premises for the relocation. Therefore the project and the planning of it should be divided into at least these two phases.

We could have two further divisions into phases. The contract phase could be divided into two: one phase leading to the requirement specifications and another from the time requirement specifications were decided upon until a contract had been signed. The first part is a pure feasibility study, while the second involves finding actual locations and selecting one of them. The relocation phase can be divided into one phase which includes the physical fitting out, renovation and relocation, and one phase which includes purchasing of equipment and installations.

Milestone plan for acquiring new premises

We will make the first phase, work leading to the signing of a contract, a separate sub-project and plan it as such.

This phase involves the acquisition of new premises. It is somewhat lacking in imagination to call the sub-project just that. Instead we will use the following wording: 'New premises for service, efficiency, job satisfaction and growth'.

The name illustrates the purpose of the sub-project. A new location is to be found, but at the same time the new premises will contribute to improving service, efficiency, job satisfaction and provide an opportunity for continued growth.

The goals for the sub-project are not identical with the goals for the project. The sub-project will only bring the project a bit further along the way to completion.

The sub-project must find suitable premises in the right surroundings. In the course of the sub-project a legally and financially satisfactory contract should be signed. In addition, the company must clarify what it needs to do to improve customer relations and the implications of this for premise requirements and choice of location. Similarly there should be an evaluation of ways of improving efficiency within the company, and what will be the related requirements for the premises to support this.

On the basis of this, we decide on four result paths:

- Premises and location.
- Economic, financial and legal matters.
- Customer service.
- Efficiency.

We formulate the goals for the sub-project which correspond to the result paths.

- Good premises and easy accessibility, opportunities for growth, good visibility.
- Select a satisfactory long- and short-term economical, financial and legal solution.
- It should be easy to be our customer.
- Good work processes, close cooperation and use of common resources.

These goals could also be presented on the milestone plan, so that they are clearly visible.

We enter 'Customer service' and 'Premises and location' as the two middle result paths in the milestone plan as we can see without detailed evaluation that these paths deal with the most central aspects of the project. The dependent relationships in the project are therefore such that it is sensible to place them in the middle. The Financial path should be placed next to the Premises path. It seems natural to place the Efficiency path next to the Customer Service path.

For practical work on milestone planning we use the form for a milestone plan shown in Figure 4.10.

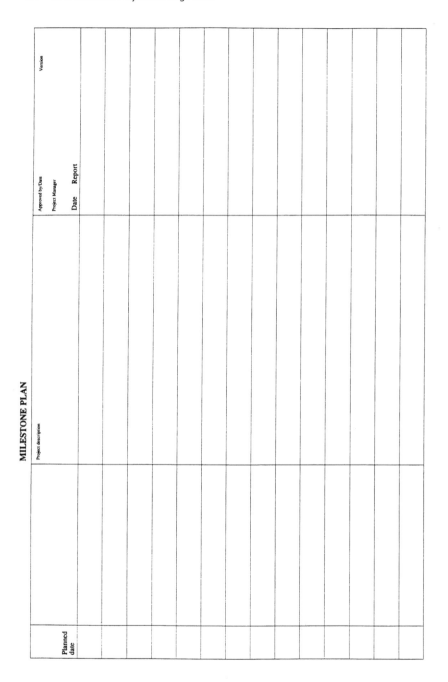

Figure 4.10 *The proforma for the milestone plan*

The milestone plan for the example sub-project is shown in Figure 4.11. The milestone plan itself is presented in the central field of the form. The plan shows the various result paths and the dependencies between the milestones. The milestones are described in the column to the right of the actual milestone plan. In order to maintain a clear overview of the plan and to facilitate later reporting, one line should be used for each milestone. One milestone can cover several result paths. In our example we can see that in order to be able to prioritise alternative locations, they must be evaluated with respect to how the requirements for service and the opportunities for efficiency are satisfied. Consequently the milestone includes both EC2 and CS2.

We can see that the form provides an opportunity to state completion dates for each milestone. This is also used for reporting. We will return to this use of the form.

It is useful to study the milestone formulations. In addition to the description of the state itself, we can include conditions and requirements for achieving the milestone. Alternatively, the conditions can be drawn up as milestones in their own right.

Milestone CS1 says: 'Customer service requirements for new premises are specified on the basis of an approved objective breakdown structure'. In order to obtain a clear picture of what the project should do for the company, we have to describe the objectives of the project in a better way. The approved objective breakdown structure could be a separate milestone. In the milestone plan we have chosen to have it as a condition in CS1.

The conditions set the work's quality standards and can also refer to methods of evaluation. By stating that an approved objective breakdown structure should exist (we show how to do this in Chapter 10) we set quality requirements which must be met before a milestone can be said to have been reached.

It is important that the milestones are formulated so that it is possible to ascertain that they have been reached.

Moreover, it is important that the milestone plan be complete. It should cover all aspects of the project. What we choose as checkpoints (milestones) is a question of expediency. They will reflect what we wish to focus on in the project. We have limited

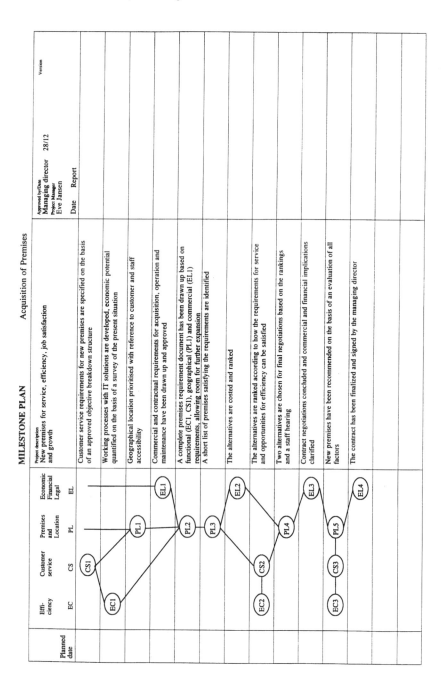

Figure 4.11 *Milestone plan for the sub-project 'New premises for service, efficiency, job satisfaction and growth'*

room, and we must weed out some milestones to obtain an easily comprehensible plan.

In the milestone plan in Figure 4.11 the expected time for completion of the different milestones is not stated for the time being. This will be done after setting up a responsibility chart and discussing who is to be responsible for realising the different milestones. We will return to this.

The milestone plan in Figure 4.11 contains 12 milestones (some of them involving several result paths). Most readers of the plan would agree that it is clearly set out, even if the project tackles a difficult set of problems (finding new premises at the same time as determining what will provide improved customer service and efficiency). Dividing the plan into four result paths contributes to creating a clear overview. It would probably be possible to insert more milestones into the plan and still maintain clarity, but there is a distinct upper limit on the number of milestones that can be included.

Milestone plan for relocation

We will make the relocation phase the second sub-project in the project. Let us take a look at a possible milestone plan for it.

The purpose of showing this plan is to demonstrate that it has a different character and distinct result paths from the milestone plan for the previous sub-project.

We do not need to wait until a contract has been concluded (milestone EL4) to start planning this sub-project. It may start immediately after a recommendation has been made (EC3, CS3, PL5). In all probability the recommendation will be followed and you will then gain time. Obviously, however, there is also the risk of wasted planning if the managing director does not approve the recommendation.

We name this sub-project 'Service, quality and teamwork in new premises'. The premises have been selected. We now wish to focus on achieving service, quality and teamwork. We do not emphasise relocation in the name. This is of secondary importance. Instead, we put the spotlight on what we want to happen in the new premises.

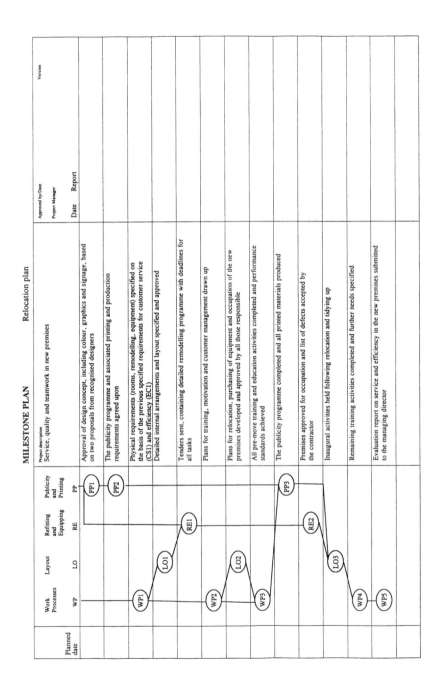

Figure 4.12 *Milestone plan for the sub-project 'Service, quality and teamwork in new premises'*

This sub-project has different goals and different result paths from the first sub-project. It should focus on:

❑ Establishing work processes and conditions for teamwork which will help the company achieve the customer service and efficiency made possible by the merging and coordination of the three divisions at the new premises.
❑ Determining the appropriate layout and equipment for the new premises.
❑ Moving into the new premises of an agreed quality at an agreed time and price.
❑ Providing information to customers about the new premises, including choice of design, use of colour and signs.

Consequently, we have four result paths:

❑ Work processes.
❑ Layout.
❑ Refitting and equipping.
❑ Publicity and printing.

The milestone plan for this sub-project is shown in Figure 4.12.

We can see from the milestone plan that milestone RE1 says that a tender for refitting is issued while RE2 states that the premises are approved for relocation. These milestones are not sufficient to guarantee good control of the remodelling work. Therefore, refitting and equipping the premises must be managed by establishing a separate sub-project. The two milestones RE1 and RE2 will be the connection between the renovation project and the 'relocation project'. This example demonstrates that it may be necessary to detail parts of a milestone plan using a separate sub-project.

5

Organising – the Project Responsibility Chart and the Principle Responsibility Chart

At the beginning of the previous chapter we introduced the different reasons for planning; planning provides an understanding of the project task, an overview of the work to be carried out, a basis for allocating and committing resources and a basis for distribution of work. Several of these factors are linked to factors which also contribute to good project organisation. Consequently, milestone planning is also important as a basis for organising the project.

In this chapter we will first present our views on how a project should be organised. We then discuss whether the hierarchical or the matrix organisational structure is most appropriate as a model for organising projects. Our conclusion is that we have the most to benefit from the matrix organisational structure. A responsibility chart is a tool which makes it possible to use the positive aspects of the matrix structure so we give a general description of a responsibility chart.

Discussions about organisation should also be divided into two stages. Organisational principles should be discussed separately from the concrete distribution of work tasks to people. The project responsibility chart and the principle responsibility chart, which are tools we use in global project organisation, are presented and we illustrate how to time schedule a project.

ASPECTS OF PROJECT ORGANISATION

Project work often requires participation by people who are not usually accustomed to this type of work. When they take part in project work, they only spend a portion of their working hours on it; that is to say they are not 100 per cent occupied with project activities. Work of this nature and with this type of effort must be organised in a certain way if the project work is to be completed without stumbling into pitfalls. Our views on important aspects of project work organisation follow.

Integration

When a project has to be organised, you quickly encounter the following problem. Should people who are to participate in project work be fully released from their other daily duties for as long as the project lasts and be physically relocated to a 'project room'? Or, while they work on the project, should they still occupy their normal work station and divide their time between project work and daily duties?

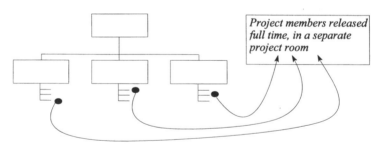

A. Project members are released from their daily work and moved

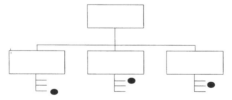

B. Project tasks are executed along with daily work. Project members remain at their desks working in their normal environment

Figure 5.1 *Two different ways of organising project work when using project members from the base organisation*

Figure 5.1 illustrates the problem. Both solutions have their advantages and their drawbacks. A solution involving a division of time between project tasks and daily tasks is termed 'integration of the project work and the base organisation', and is represented by B in Figure 5.1.

The advantage of releasing people from other tasks and moving them to a 'project room', represented by A in Figure 5.1, is that the project member can concentrate completely on project work. Nothing else disturbs him and it is possible for him to concentrate fully on the project.

When people are moved to the project room it does not usually take very long before they see things from the project's point of view and lose the perspective of the base organisation. When, for example, user representatives are included in a computer systems development project on a full-time basis, they often very quickly become 'computer people' and begin to talk 'computerese'. This is one of alternative A's drawbacks. The project members cease to be concerned with the very interests which they are placed in the project to represent. Another drawback is poor utilization of resources, especially in projects where progress depends on decisions from the base organisation. Since project members no longer work so closely with their home location, these decisions are often delayed.

The advantage of B is that in principle the whole base organisation is at the disposal of project tasks. Not having to pull people who will perform project tasks out of the base organisation gives greater flexibility. You can concentrate on finding the people who have the best qualifications for the tasks and a larger number of people can be involved in the work. Some may do a very limited amount of work while others may work nearly full-time for a period.

In B, the project will be regarded as the responsibility of the base organisation to a greater extent. Project members remain at their own desks and do not lose their links with their usual job and their area of expertise.

Integration of project work into the base organisation means that you need to gain acceptance for the fact that development tasks (which projects are) are also an important activity for people who have a job in the ordinary base organisation. This integration generally leads to a more positive attitude towards development work in the base organisation.

When the project is integrated, there is in addition a tendency for people other than the individual project members to become engaged in project problems and progress. Naturally enough, project members discuss their problems and successes with their colleagues, producing increased involvement in the project.

Alternative B also makes it easier for a project member to take up small matters with colleagues. The probability of an informal hearing is greater when people have easy access to colleagues. If someone is taken out of the base organisation, completely different procedures must be used to gather in opinions from his original environment.

Alternative B provides a more effective use of resources. It is easier to utilize spare time if you are in your normal work environment. You can simply turn to your other duties. There is a danger in alternative A that the project manager will attempt to fill free time by assigning tasks which are not ready to be done or assigning tasks to a person not qualified to carry them out.

You can deduce from this that we are in favour of alternative B. We do not deny, however, that it may be difficult to implement. An absolutely essential prerequisite is that the terms of responsibility and authority have been clearly set out and detailed in advance. It is unrealistic to believe that integration of project work into the base organisation will be achieved without prior agreement and understanding.

Three particularly important factors must be evaluated before integrating project work into the base organisation can be recommended.

❑ *The line manager's qualities:* it is especially important to assess whether the line manager will manage to organise his department in such a way that project members can be relieved of their normal operational tasks to the extent agreed upon.

❑ *The project members' qualities:* an assessment must be made as to whether project members will manage to combine their normal tasks and project tasks while giving the agreed priority to the project. There are certain people who need to be supervised constantly; if not, they will always be fully occupied with their normal job instead of project work.

❑ *The environment in the base organisation:* at the outset there must be acceptance in the base organisation of the fact that colleagues will spend a certain amount of their time on project work. If there is no such acceptance, the environment will hamper the project members' ability to perform their project tasks. They will never have the peace from customers, colleagues, or management necessary to do the project work. Colleagues must also agree to relieve the project members of some of their normal duties.

We believe that alternative B is the best – when it is feasible. When a project member is sitting in the base organisation and is performing project work, it must be permissible for him to let his colleagues know this and that consequently he should not be disturbed with daily matters at this time. Everyone should respect this.

We reiterate, however, that when a person is to divide his time among various types of tasks, it is a prerequisite that procedures for handling conflicts of priority be clarified and established in advance.

Principal organisational matters before details

When working on project organisation you often become very concerned with the question of who will perform the various project tasks. Of course, it is important to fill all the posts in a project with able people. However, as when planning project work, there is a tendency to become too quickly involved in discussing the details (in this case choice of personnel and distribution of work tasks) before the global principles are made clear.

Distinguishing between the global principles for the participation and roles of the various parties involved in the project, and the actual allocation of tasks to specific people, is an important aspect of good organisation.

In discussing principles, decisions are made about what role the different parties concerned will play in the project. In this discussion, the project, the base organisation and other parties involved agree upon the 'rules of the game'. Such discussions of principle are especially important when the project will draw on resources from the base organisation. (This applies in most projects, apart from huge projects where everyone is engaged full-time on the project.) This is particularly important when the project work is integrated into the base organisation. It is necessary to clarify the organisation's responsibility for and participation in the project and this must be done before you begin to consider people for the project tasks.

Clarification of all roles and responsibilities

Every project has relationships with many different parties. Examples of these parties are proposers of the project, the users of the project results (both the line management and the end users) and other interested bodies (for example a trade union).

In a PSO project which is developing a computer-based ordering and invoicing system, for example, the parties involved are the company's top management, the finance director (the 'user boss'), members of the finance department (the users), members of the computer department (different types of experts), trade unions, and the company's major suppliers and customers. When organising the project, both the principles governing relationships between the parties involved and the practical consequences of these relationships must be defined. It must be clear who will make the different types of decisions, who should be informed, and who should perform the different types of work. Through such careful definition, organisational pitfalls can be avoided.

In a traditional project organisation, the terms of responsibility and authority are described for those who have formal connections with the project. We do not want to detract from the importance of outlining clear guidelines for responsibility and authority internally within the project – to the contrary. At the same time we stress the importance of clarifying relationships with all other parties involved in the project. This is often neglected when setting up a project.

Defining decision-making responsibilities

Part of organising a project is to clarify which types of decisions will be taken by the various parties involved. We maintain as a principle point of departure that decisions should be taken by those in the base organisation who are normally responsible for these kinds of decisions.

If a computer-based invoicing system is to be drawn up, it will contain rules for discount. These must be formulated. When there are people in the base organisation who have daily responsibility for determining this sort of thing, why should they not continue to have it? Why should the right to make this type of decision be transferred to a steering committee, a project group or some computer people because the work of developing and implementing the new system is organised as a project? The person responsible for the area of concern should be responsible for taking decisions which affect that area, and he should do this by virtue of his job in the base organisation. However, these demands on the line manager or his subordinates must be defined and agreed upon when setting up the project. Otherwise there is a great danger that the project will usurp the power to make decisions. The consequence of this is that at a later stage the base organisation will deny responsibility for the system, because they – and rightly so – will point to the fact that it is the project that has made the decisions which should have been made by the base organisation.

There is always a tendency for a project steering committee to become a project decision group and make decisions which it does not have the qualifications or the right to make. We strongly reject the idea that such a group function as decision-makers concerning professional questions. A project must not deprive the base organisation of its responsibility for making professionally-related decisions.

Communicating effectively

In some projects the problem of information is resolved by disseminating mountains of information about the project to anyone who may be considered to have an interest in it. The problem of consultation is resolved by assembling people in reference groups. For fear of treading on someone's toes, too few or too many are included in these groups. The consequence of this is meetings where many of those present are not responsible for or have no connection with the problems discussed. Reference groups often serve as a form of collective hostage.

We recommend more careful consideration of whom should be consulted and informed. This is desirable both with regard to the administrative work the project will otherwise take upon itself in widespread and uncritical dissemination of information, and with regard to the results it will achieve. It is better to have some thorough discussions with individuals than superficial discussions in a large reference group.

Flexibility

In many projects a project group will be formally appointed, consisting of the group of people who will carry out the work involved in the project. These people are there from start to finish, and will perform all the large and small tasks in the project. This is a dangerous form of organisation. When we have a project organisation where people are formally assigned to a project for its lifetime, we will find that we:

- have problems varying the input of resources during the lifetime of the project;
- are precluded from using the best line people for certain tasks;
- create a gap between those who are formally included in the project and those who are not.

It is important to be organised in such a way that the project has flexibility to acquire different types of resources at different stages of the project. We call this an accordion-type organisation. At the same time it is important that we state precisely what each individual should do.

With an accordion-type organisation we achieve the following:

- The number of people working on the project can vary in its lifetime. This is an advantage because during the course of a project the requirement for an input of resources and different types of expertise varies considerably.
- The 'right' expertise is crucial when allocating tasks, and we have a better chance to get this expertise when the project is organised more flexibly. When project members are formally appointed to cover all project jobs, we are prevented from using the most competent people in the base organisation when needed. Of course, even with a formally appointed project group we can still get help from people outside the project. However, they are not a part of the project in the same formal way. When they agree to do a job, they often do it as an act of friendship; we are dependent on their goodwill. It is important that everyone working on a project has the same status within it.
- Participation in the project always depends on whether or not the person in question is presently doing a job for the project. A flexible form of organisation means that participation in the project is in a constant state of flux. Permanent appointments create rigidity and management difficulties. The project will be obliged to hang on to people who no longer have anything to do. We have yet to see an internal memo stating that a person is leaving the formal project group and is no longer participating in a project.

HIERARCHY OR MATRIX?

How then should you organise a project? A hierarchical organisation is often used and recommended when organising a project. Figure 5.2 shows a project organisation where the hierarchical structure forms the basis.

We say, a little in jest, that this recommendation is the greatest disaster to strike project work. An uncritical use of a hierarchical structure inevitably leads to problems.

For very large and long-term projects which work on isolated tasks and are staffed mainly by full-time employees, the hierarchical structure may be appropriate. But it is not good when the project is to be integrated with the base organisation, and will therefore, to a great extent, affect and involve people in large sections of that organisation.

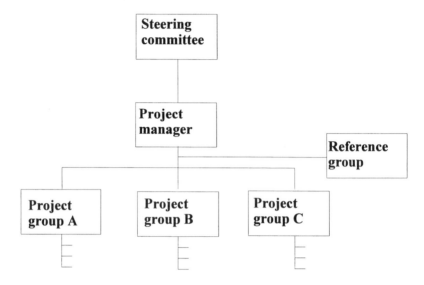

Figure 5.2 *A project organised according to the hierarchical (bureaucratic) structure*

The strength of a hierarchical structure is that it describes the responsibilities of the organisational units which appear on the organisation chart. It shows the chains of command between different units in an organisation. This method of organisation, however, has many built-in limitations with regard to what we expect from good project organisation.

The hierarchical structure does not make clear something upon which it is very important to agree, namely the relationship between the project and all parties involved, the base organisation in particular. Instead, the hierarchical model fosters concern with the project's internal structure.

When the relationship with groups and individuals within the base organisation is not clarified, the result is a collapse of authority – it is not clear who is responsible for what. This can often lead to the project usurping responsibility for matters outside its jurisdiction on the grounds of 'getting things done'.

The principle that professional decisions follow the normal decision-making process in the organisation will easily be broken in this context. Instead, the hierarchical structure promotes bureaucratic procedures in the project, with several levels included in the decision process.

The hierarchical structure also makes flexible use of resources difficult. It does not invite commitment from people outside the project. It is also difficult to achieve informal communication, because this structure actually emphasises set and formalised lines of communication.

We are generally against organising projects according to the hierarchical structure. Figure 5.3 summarises our views.

Organising a project according to the hierarchical structure often leads to
- bureaucracy
- inefficiency
- poor use of resources
- collapse of authority or the project usurping responsibility it should not have
- little commitment from people outside the project
- little informal contact between the project and its surroundings

---

Figure 5.3 *Possible negative effects of organising a project according to the hierarchical structure*

What, then, is the alternative? Our recommendation draws inspiration from the matrix. In a matrix organisation, groups and individuals are arranged in various constellations of responsibility and authority, depending on the matter involved. This is the organisational aspect we want to utilise in projects.

The matrix structure is used, for example, in companies which sell several types of product and which are established in several regions. Such a company may have a regional organisation, where each region has a regional director, a regional management and staff in a set hierarchy. But in addition the company has an organisational division according to product, with a product manager for each product having authority also over the regional staff who are connected with that product. The workers are therefore subordinate to the regional director in matters such as those concerning work in the region, and to the product manager in others such as technical product questions and marketing.

A matrix organisation eases communication between groups and individuals who need to cooperate. There are shorter lines of communication than in a hierarchical structure. This should in its turn lead to better decisions and a better utilisation of the organisation's human resources.

In Figure 5.4 we have summarised the essential advantages of using a matrix model. It also has drawbacks. The organisation of projects that we suggest is not a typical matrix organisation; therefore we choose to say that we have taken inspiration from the matrix structure and used its favourable aspects.

Organising a project based on relevant aspects of the matrix structure often leads to
- a better structure for decision-making and responsibility
- better communication through shorter lines of communication
- a more flexible organisation, better adjusted to the problem and the people who will work on it
- better use of resources

Figure 5.4 *Essential advantages of using the matrix structure as the basis for organising a project*

RESPONSIBILITY CHARTS

Purpose

The project organisation should be 'tailor made' to resolve the project task. Because every project is unique, it is important that an organisation be specially formulated for each individual project. It should be as suitable as possible with regard to the task to be performed.

To reiterate, we should pay attention, when organising, to the important matters briefly summed up as follows. We must have an accordion-type organisation, where people are included in a project only as long as they have tasks to perform. We must always observe the principle that the right to make decisions on professionally-related questions belongs to those who have daily responsibility for them. Project work must be integrated into the base organisation. The right people must be consulted and informed.

Our method of organising projects requires a thorough discussion of what the people involved in the project (project management, project members, line management, users, shop stewards, etc) will do. Discussions on organisation must occur at two levels, ie the clarification of organisational principles before dealing with detailed matters.

Establishing a 'tailor made' project organisation requires that a fundamental stance be taken on what roles the various parties involved should play in the project at the global level. The 'rules of the game' which will apply to the project should be clarified.

Detailed organisation – which comes at a later stage – requires clarification of which concrete activities will be performed, and the commitment that specific people will have to the different activities.

Both discussions – the global discussion and the detail discussion – will be held with the help of a tool which we call a *responsibility chart*. The responsibility chart is inspired by the matrix model, and is sometimes called a responsibility matrix or a responsibility contract.

The responsibility chart is constructed in the same way whether we are on the global level (drawing up a project responsibility chart and principle responsibility chart) or on the detail level (activity responsibility chart). But the charts clarify different types of questions. The project responsibility chart and the principle responsibility chart explain and describe the roles of the different parties in important project matters. The activity responsibility chart explains and describes the roles of specific people in concrete project activities. Figure 5.5 illustrates a responsibility chart.

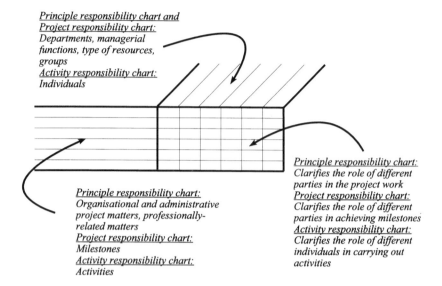

Principle responsibility chart and
Project responsibility chart:
Departments, managerial
functions, type of resources,
groups
Activity responsibility chart:
Individuals

Principle responsibility chart:
Organisational and administrative
project matters, professionally-
related matters
Project responsibility chart:
Milestones
Activity responsibility chart:
Activities

Principle responsibility chart:
Clarifies the role of different
parties in the project work
Project responsibility chart:
Clarifies the role of different
parties in achieving milestones
Activity responsibility chart:
Clarifies the role of different
individuals in carrying out
activities

Figure 5.5 *Responsibility chart*

Roles

The responsibility charts will also be used to clarify roles, at
both global and detail levels.

Roles are the same at both levels. Figure 5.6 shows the different roles and the abbreviations which will be used on the
responsibility chart.

The responsibility chart makes it possible to mark who
should 'do the job', ie be in charge of executing a specific task.

We can also state who will make decisions on a matter. We
have two different decision symbols. We differentiate between
principal and subsidiary decision-making. A problem can very
often be divided into subsidiary problems, and the authority to
make decisions can be divided accordingly. One makes the
global decision (or 'has the final word'). The authority to make
decisions on different subsidiary problems and the responsibility
for these decisions may belong to different people or parties.
The division into major decisions and subsidiary decisions
makes it possible for upper management to hand over subsidiary
decisions to others.

X   Executes the work

D   Takes decisions solely or ultimately
d   Takes decisions jointly or partly

P   Manages work and controls progress

T   Provides tuition on the job

C   Must be consulted
I   Must be informed
A   Available to advise

Figure 5.6 *Roles in a project identified on the responsibility charts with their abbreviations*

Figure 5.7 further illustrates the use and interpretation of the decision symbols. We stress that there cannot be two capital 'D's on the same line, apart from cases where the project is a joint effort between two or more independent organisations. There is only one person in an organisation who can have the overall responsibility for a decision. However, there may well be several lower case 'd's on the same line. If there are only lower case 'd's – without a capital 'D' – it means that the 'd' people must agree and make decisions jointly. If, on the other hand, in addition to small 'd's there is a capital 'D', it implies that the 'D' person is included in the decision-making process and has the final responsibility.

In certain cases the decision symbols stand for professional approval. We have not found it necessary to have a separate symbol for this. This is evident from the context when a decision is made, and when the situation is more a case of professional approval.

On the responsibility chart one can show whether a group or an individual 'must be consulted'. This does not mean that the person concerned has veto powers, but that it is a very serious mistake if the person concerned is not allowed to express his/her views. This symbol is often used to describe the role of a trade union representative or an accountant. Neither has the authority

	Party X	Party Y	Party Z	Explanation
Example I	D			X has full responsibility for the decision
Example II	D	d		Y answers for professional quality and gives approval within his field. X has full responsibility for the decision
Example III	D	d	d	Y and Z agree jointly, but X makes the formal decision
Example IV		d	d	If Y and Z agree jointly, their decision stands. If not, the decision is taken at a higher level in the management hierarchy

Figure 5.7 *Use of decision symbols in a responsibility chart*

to make decisions or veto power, but it is important to listen to their opinions, and they weigh heavily when decisions are to be made.

'Available for advice' is used for several reasons. It is used to open up channels of communication in extremely formal surroundings. An 'A' implies the formal opportunity to 'pester people'. Those involved understand that they can be contacted to discuss problems. The symbol can also be used to indicate that here are people with particular expertise on which it may be important to draw. Otherwise it is easy to overlook this expertise when there is a job to be done. Accountants are a good example of this. People who are assigned the 'A' symbol thus receive a formal role in the project. This sign can be particularly important when there are external consultants involved in the project. It gives these consultants a right to make contact with people in the base organisation without having to ask someone for permission. Gathering information and establishing contact can be otherwise difficult for consul-tants who come from outside the organisation. If 'available for advice' is marked against an external consultant, it implies that the project has a green light for use of consultants.

'Must be informed' is important because it forces a discussion of who should be informed about what in the project.

Responsibility for work and progress is marked with a capital 'P'. In project work where we are constantly struggling both to achieve high quality and to keep within time limits and budget, responsibility for progress is especially important. It implies executing the management functions of planning, organisation and control over the work of project members.

There should always be one capital 'P' on each line of the responsibility chart. There must always be one, and only one, person who is responsible for the progress of the task concerned.

On the responsibility chart we can mark the responsibility for transfer of knowledge with a capital 'T'. It involves a combination of leadership and support when performing the job. At the start of a task, the people who will perform it do not always have the expertise to do it on their own, and must acquire this expertise. This, for example, is the case when an actual situation has to be described using a special investigation method or descriptive technique and those performing the task do not have adequate knowledge of that technique. It is then necessary that training and support be given during the course of the work.

In general we would like to suggest that you should be sparing in the use of symbols on responsibility charts. If the responsibility chart is showered with symbols, there will be consequences for the length of the project. In such cases there should be a new round of discussions on the responsibility chart to decide whether such broad involvement is really desirable. If broad involvement is desired then so be it but everyone must realise that this will slow down the progress of the project.

The working out of the responsibility chart – both at global and detail levels – requires thorough discussion. The responsibility chart gives a condensed description of what has been agreed upon. There is sometimes a need to supplement the responsibility chart with a verbal description, where the significance of the individual symbols in the matrix is dealt with in more depth.

The discussion will result in an appropriate project organisation. However, the clarification process which must take place to produce an organisational pattern is just as important as the end result.

In organisational work all parties involved at the global level and all individuals involved at the detail level must be included. The relationships to the project of each party and each individual are clarified in the discussion. Any disagreements on the understanding of or expectations to individual roles can be taken up and resolved. This will not eradicate all conflicts in a project, but undoubtedly a range of problems which could later have broken out into open conflict will be forestalled at an early stage.

A further benefit, and not the least, is that cooperation on organising a project also leads to those involved identifying themselves with it. Loyalty to the project and to commitments will be created.

COMPREHENSIVE PROJECT ORGANISATION

At the global level we bring up and clarify three areas of responsibility:

❏ Achievement of the various milestones in the milestone plan.
❏ Tasks of an organisational or administrative nature.
❏ Professional matters (eg legal, computing, technical).

Who should be responsible for the project achieving the different milestones in the milestone plan depends on the project. The division of responsibility is therefore only valid for the specific project being worked on. The description of responsibility for achieving milestones in one project is unique and we cannot use it in any other project. We therefore call such a responsibility chart the project responsibility chart.

The two other conditions to be clarified at the global level are, however, of a more general nature. The areas of responsibility set out here may be valid for all projects in the organisation. Consequently they express principles which may apply both to this project and to any other projects. We therefore call the responsibility chart which shows these areas of responsibility a principle responsibility chart.

The project responsibility chart

We will begin by discussing responsibility for achieving milestones. The project responsibility chart can be regarded as a contract between the project and the parties involved. It is important in this contract to agree upon the relationships between those involved and the project, and that the 'frontiers' between those involved are staked out where necessary. In a project, management and members from the base organisation are drawn in. For the project to be successful it is necessary that all parties involved in the base organisation understand clearly what responsibilities they have and accept them explicitly.

A quite natural extension of milestone planning is the discussion about who should be responsible for the different milestones. In practice we take each milestone in turn, discuss them, decide upon which parties should play a role in achieving them, and agree upon the role of these parties.

When we discussed the milestone plan, we first showed a very simple plan for the project of drawing up an action plan to improve the work environment in a business. (It would be a good idea to look at Figure 4.7 again.) We saw later that a milestone plan is usually more extensive, but this first plan played a role as a simple introduction to the milestone plan concept. We will now show in Figure 5.8 what the project responsibility chart might look like for this task.

In a milestone plan, each milestone is formulated as a description of a state, possibly with certain conditions attached. It is work leading up to the milestones that will be regulated on the responsibility chart. We do not, therefore, repeat the whole milestone formula. We can select a formulation which clearly shows that it is the work up to the milestone that we are looking at. Or we can use keywords from the milestone and let it be understood that the responsibility chart applies to the responsibility for achieving that milestone.

	Project manager	Managing director	Affected line managers	Personnel consultant	Work environment commitee	External consultant
M1 Description of present situation	X/P	A	C	X	X	T
M2 Description of desired situation	X/P	D	d	X	C	
M3 Requirements for change	X/P			X	I	
M4 Ideas for measures	X/P		C	X	C	A
M5 Consequences of the measures	X/P		X		I	
M6 Action plan	X/P		C	X	C	

Figure 5.8 *Project responsibility chart for a project which will draw up an action plan to improve the work environment*

Milestone M1 is called 'When there is a description of the present situation'. On the project responsibility chart it says 'Description of present situation'. These are keywords from the complete milestone formulation. 'Describe the present situation' could also be entered there. Such a term indicates more clearly that it is the responsibility for the work to achieve the milestone which will be agreed upon.

Some milestones say something about who should make decisions, or who should confirm that a milestone has been achieved. It is unnecessary to repeat this in the keywords on the responsibility chart because this is exactly what the responsibility chart shows – eg where the authority to make decisions lies.

Now and again it is necessary to divide a milestone into two or more sections on the responsibility chart because the authority relationships are so different. If the milestone is seen as one unit, these differences are not perceived.

In the above example we could have divided M5 'Consequences of the measures' into two parts, one part called 'Economic consequences of the measures' and another part called 'Consequences of the measures on the work environment'. The responsibility chart could thus have shown that the parties participating in the work on investigating the economic consequences will not be the same as those who investigate the effects on the work environment. In the example we have not gone into the tasks in great depth; in practice this is often necessary.

The project responsibility chart shows what responsibility the different parties have for realising the milestones. This responsibility can thus consist of being responsible for progress, executing work, making decisions, being available for consultation, receiving information or tutoring. A party may well have several roles simultaneously. It is usual, for example, at least in smaller projects, that the person responsible for progress also participates in doing actual project work.

It is sometimes difficult to find suitable terms for the parties involved, especially when responsibility will be assigned to a group of people who are not usually regarded as forming *one* unit. The realisation of a milestone may, for example, require a specific effort from certain, but not all, line managers. In such cases the group may be called 'affected line managers', 'specific line managers' or something similar.

In the example we see that affected line managers 'must be consulted' in the description of the present situation. This means that the head of production must make a statement on the actual situation in the production department, the head of marketing on the situation in the marketing department, the head of personnel on the situation in the personnel department, etc. When it is stated that the affected line manager should make a subsidiary decision on the desired situation, it means that the head of production will decide on matters for his department, the head of marketing for his, and so on. But we see that the managing director makes the principal decision. This means that the director has the right to reconsider whatever the line managers have decided.

It is important to realise that one person may be included in several parties. For example, one person may be both an elected employee representative and an affected user. The responsibilities attached to each of these functions are essentially different, and this may lead to the person being assigned different types of work on the basis of his affiliation with different groups.

A further evaluation of the milestone plan is made during work on the project responsibility chart. If there are any logical flaws, problems may occur in filling in the responsibility chart. It may indeed be the case that work on the responsibility chart will lead you to return to, reassess, and alter the milestone plan.

Discussing responsibilities is not an easy process. It is important, as we also said in connection with the development of the milestone plan, to arrange matters practically so that all participants can engage in a genuine group discussion. We pointed out earlier that use of an overhead projector and a white-board in presentations ensures that everyone can follow the discussion towards agreement. In addition, these tools make it easy to note down changes.

We usually recommend that the discussion about roles and responsibilities start by considering the first three or four milestones and the different parties involved. If there are no problems, then all the subsequent milestones can be set up. The reason that we recommend that you start with a few milestones is that it can be difficult to establish which parties should be included on the responsibility chart, and it is unnecessary to discuss all the milestones before you feel that you have found the right ones.

When the project responsibility chart has been developed, it is useful to evaluate the results. Two types of analyses can be made:

❏ Horizontal analysis.
❏ Vertical analysis.

In the horizontal analysis each milestone is taken separately and the work to achieve each one is evaluated. You should assess if the roles have been correctly balanced and integrated for the milestone. We have emphasised earlier that there must be one person who is responsible for managing progress. It is easy to check whether this requirement is satisfied. There are larger problems in determining whether there is sufficient skill and expertise among those executing the work. You might assess at this point whether there is a need for on-the-job training and whether the right advice can be obtained from those whom one can or must consult. The group must consider whether decisions are held at the right level. It must also determine whether too many or too few are being informed.

In the vertical analysis the total load placed on those involved in the project is assessed for each party separately. There must be a discussion about whether it has taken on too much. It may also be considered if the party has too modest a role in the project. Instead of being available for consultation, the party should, for example, perhaps also be assigned task execution.

A form consisting of three sections has been drawn up for a responsibility chart. It is shown in Figure 5.9. The form has:

❑ a responsibility section;
❑ an activity schedule section;
❑ a progress report section.

We will begin by using the responsibility section, and will return to the schedule and the report sections.

Example of a project responsibility chart

We will continue with the project 'Improved customer service and more efficient operation in new premises'. We will look at the first sub-project: 'New premises for service, efficiency, job satisfaction and growth'. The milestone plan for this sub-project was shown in Figure 4.11. Figure 5.10 shows the project responsibility chart which corresponds to the milestone plan.

The project responsibility chart is presented on a standard form, which can be used for all types of responsibility charts. The chart presents the responsibilities for realising the milestone plan. In this project we talk about three categories of resources in the milestone plan. They are:

❑ The line management and other members of the base organisation.
❑ The project manager and project members.
❑ External resources.

It is important that the base organisation be drawn into the project. It is not possible to achieve better service and efficiency in the new premises if the base organisation is not deeply

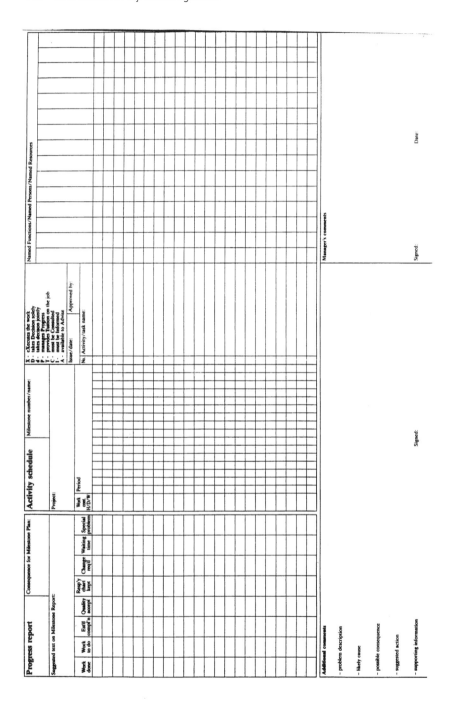

Figure 5.9 *The proforma for the responsibility chart*

PROJECT RESPONSIBILITY CHART — Acquisition of Premises

Key:
- X - executes the work
- D - takes decision solely
- d - takes decision jointly
- P - manages progress
- T - provides tuition on the job
- C - must be consulted
- I - must be informed
- A - available to advise

Approved by/Date: Managing director   28/12   Version

Column legend:
1 Managing director · 2 Head of Finance · 3 Head of Personnel · 4 Head of Marketing · 5 Affected Line Manager · 6 Affected Staff · 7 Project Manager · 8 Team member – operation · 9 Team member – financial · 10 Team member – legal · 11 Space coordinator · 12 Union representative · 13 Consultant · 14 Real Estate Agent · 15

No.	Milestones	1	2	3	4	5	6	7	8	9	10	11	12	13	14	15
CS1	Objective Breakdown Structure	DX	X	X	X	C	C	PX	X	I	I	I	C	T		
CS1	Customer service requirements	D			dX	d	C	PX	X			I	I	C		
EC1	Work processes					d	X	PX	X			I	I	I		
EC1	Improvement potential			d	d	d	C	PX	X			I	C	A		
PL1	Location assessment	D	d			d	C	P	X							
EL1	Commercial requirements	D				C		I		PX	X		X		C	
PL2	Requirements document	D						X	I	I	I	PX	I	I		
PL2	Search specification	I				C	C	PX				I	I	I		
PL3	Premises shortlist					I		C								
EL2	Commercial assessment							PX	X	PX	X				PX	
CS2	Functional assessment	D						PX	C	C	C	C				
PL4	Two alternatives	D	d	d	d	d						C	I	I	C	
EL3	Contract negotiations		PX		C					X	X		C		C	
PL5	Recommendation	D	PX	C		I	I	I	I	I	I			C		
EL4	Contract signed	D	P					I			X				A	

Figure 5.10 *Project responsibility chart for the sub-project 'New premises for service, efficiency, job satisfaction and growth'*

involved in the project work. The responsibility chart must clearly state what roles the different parties in the base organisation will have.

Special responsibilities for the heads of finance, personnel and marketing departments are stated. We also find on the responsibility chart that all affected line managers have been given an area of responsibility. The responsibility applying to the affected line managers also applies to line managers who previously have been given a defined responsibility. The special responsibilities come in addition to that applying to all those affected by the project.

Some people from the base organisation will spend more time on the project than others. It is natural to talk about them as team members or project members, even if we emphasise that a formal project group has not been established. There is a need for project members who can work on customer service and operational matters. The project requires a member with expertise in economics and finance, who can make an economic evaluation of the alternative premises. There is also a need for legal expertise and a space coordinator. The trade union representatives have been willing to perform certain tasks exceeding their role as elected representatives, so they can also be regarded as project members.

It is relevant to draw some external assistance into the project. On the responsibility chart a space is allocated for a consultant and an estate agent.

Some milestones are divided on the responsibility chart because they consist of work that varies greatly in nature. This applies to CS1, EC1 and PL2.

The different roles on the responsibility chart are shown using the symbols discussed previously. The responsibility chart should be as self-explanatory as possible. It will be all the easier to understand if those using it have participated in the development process.

The principle responsibility chart

On the principle responsibility chart the responsibility for general project organisational and administrative matters are clarified, as well as professional matters of principle. These are matters which do not only apply to a single milestone, but which cover the whole project.

Whatever is agreed on in the principle responsibility chart can also be valid for other projects in the organisation. The base organisation may decide that these are principles which will apply to all projects.

A principle responsibility chart which encompasses all projects is of great importance for the organisation's project culture and project efficiency. It does away with the need for every individual project to discuss general project organisational and administrative matters. One can simply refer to the principle responsibility chart for projects.

Figure 5.11 shows an example of a principle responsibility chart. It illustrates which matters it is desirable to clarify using this type of responsibility chart. In the example the roles the different parties may have are also stated. We stress that what is stated in the figure is only an example and is not universally valid. Indeed, the discussion on setting up a responsibility chart involves precisely the taking of decisions on the role of the different parties in the project.

The principle responsibility chart shows who is responsible for the chart itself. The example illustrates that we feel it is appropriate for the managing director to have approved it. The principles on which project work will be run in the company should be approved by the top manager.

The principle responsibility chart also establishes who plays a role in the work on drawing up the milestone plan and the project responsibility chart. An important aspect of planning and organisation at this level is to get resources allocated to the project. The responsibility chart also shows who is responsible for this. The milestone report provides a report on the progress of the project.

	Mana-ging director	Affected director	Affected line manager	Imple-mentor	Project manager	Affected staff member	Elected repre-sentative
Principle responsibility chart	D	C	C		X/P	I	C
Milestone plan, project responsibility chart	I	D	X	X	X/P	X	I
Allocation of resources, global level	D	d	X	C	P	I	I
Milestone report		D	C	C	X/P	I	I
Activity planning binding completion date		C	C	C	X/P		
- select implementor			d	C	X/P		
- determine duration of activity					X/P	X	
- determine start time and sequence					D		
- commit line resources			d	d			
- release line resources			X/P	X			
- execute activity				X	P	C	
Activity responsibility				C	X/P		
Activity report				X	P		
Work environment matters		D	C		P	C	C

Figure 5.11 *Example of a principle responsibility chart*

We argued earlier that project work should be integrated into the base organisation. In order for this to function a process is necessary whereby the roles of the different parties are established and clarified. The principle responsibility chart shows what is a rational division of work and responsibility for the central planning tasks in such a project.

Global matters are regulated via the responsibility for drawing up a milestone plan and a project responsibility chart. After that, detailed planning can be done. It is first looked at in a general way; it is ascertained that it is the project manager's responsibility. The project manager must lead and take responsibility for activity planning. At the same time it is made clear that the line manager and those carrying out tasks must be consulted on all essential matters.

These are thus the leading roles in the detailed planning work. A further, more precise definition is given to certain important tasks. It is the project manager and the line manager who will agree jointly on who from the base organisation should perform tasks for the project. The personnel proposed must have an opportunity to give their opinion on the matter before the decision is made.

When planning project work, the resources needed for the individual activities to be executed must be evaluated. This should be done jointly by the project manager and those who will perform the activities. They should determine together how demanding on resources an activity is.

If the project manager makes the evaluation alone, it will not be binding on those who will perform the job. Unfortunately, some project managers behave somewhat tyrannically. First they commit themselves externally concerning how long an activity will take, and then they compel the implementor to accept the commitment. This can work, but usually it does not. The implementor is in a difficult position regardless of what the result is. If he does not manage to meet deadlines, he will be criticised unfairly. If he does meet them, he will be given new tasks with the same pressure.

Neither is it correct for the implementor alone to evaluate how much work an activity demands. The project manager must be included, because he has experience and because he needs the insight provided by a thorough discussion of the requirements of an activity. Some implementors are over-optimistic; then the project manager must make adjustments.

Some project managers have acquired the habit of consistently lowering the estimates of the implementor. This is a dangerous policy. In the course of time the result will be that the implementor will not feel bound by these estimates; they are looked upon as the sole responsibility of the project manager.

The ideal situation is that a good relationship based on openness and trust between the project manager and the implementor allows them to arrive at a mutual agreement on the extent of resources required to carry out the activities.

It is the project manager's responsibility, based on an assessment of the dependencies between activities in the project, to determine when an activity should be performed. The line managers and the implementors must together commit themselves to making resources available at the right time. The commitment must be mutual; neither the line manager nor the implementor can make commitments by themselves. If only one of them makes the decision, it may clash with the other's arrangements. The result will be that the resources are not available for the project when they are needed.

The project activities shall be carried out by those who have the executing responsibility. The line manager's responsibility, however, is to see to it that the implementors are released from their line duties so they can carry out project tasks. The line manager must plan his use of resources in the base organisation so that he can make them available to the project when agreed. His plan must state which members of the base organisation will take over assignments from those taking on project tasks. While doing the planning, the line manager must consult with the implementor's supervisor.

The responsibility for allocating resources to the project can be made perfectly clear, and straightforward agreements may be reached. Nevertheless, it is sometimes difficult to implement these agreements in practice. A generally positive climate must be created for the use of resources for development work. All the plans and agreements in the world will be of no use if they are not supported by the people in the base organisation.

Situations may arise which make it necessary to re-evaluate the project plan and the allocation of resources for the project. The project plan is not a 'sacred cow' which cannot be touched. Conditions may arise which are so important that changes to the plan must be accepted.

Let us say that a computer-based invoicing system is to be installed in a company. There are two people in the accounts department, and it is agreed that one of them should be released part-time to participate in developing the new invoicing system. But then the other person falls ill. There is then a choice between keeping to the project plan and stopping company invoicing for a time, or continuing to invoice and letting the project plan fall apart. In such situations it is obvious that priorities and plans for the project must be reassessed.

Changes to the plan must thus be accepted. The important point is that a system is in place which can discover at an early stage that the plans are not being adhered to. Then there is a chance to introduce measures to set a new course.

We will discuss this in more detail in the chapter on control. The principle responsibility chart states that it is the implementor's responsibility to draw up the activity reports on project progress. They provide the project manager with the basis for drawing up the milestone reports which show where the project is in relation to the project milestones.

On the principle responsibility chart we can also show who is responsible for making decisions on professionally-related matters which may arise in the project. The general principle is that decisions should be made by whoever is responsible for these fields in the line. However, it may sometimes be useful to define precisely how professional questions should be handled. An example of how work environment questions should be handled is shown on the responsibility chart in Figure 5.11.

TIME SCHEDULING AND RESOURCE ESTIMATION

Time scheduling is an important aspect of project planning. We have two different situations:

❑ The completion date is set by the proposer or determined by matters beyond the organisation's control.
❑ The project will work out a realistic completion date itself.

An imposed completion date is a situation that a project must accept. There may be several reasons for it, for example:

❑ The project is based on a strategic decision in the base organisation which requires a specific completion date.
❑ The completion date is based on market considerations. (Because of the market situation the results of the project must be available by a specific date.)
❑ The project is a sub-project in a larger project. (If the results of the project are not available by a specific date, other projects will be delayed.)
❑ The completion date is set through a decision by public authorities.
❑ The results of the project will be used in the organisation's annual planning cycle, and as a result of this they must be available by a specific date.

We will look first at the situation where the project itself will suggest a completion date.

In practice we find that many projects commit themselves to a specific deadline on grounds which are too loosely defined. Such a point in time has a tendency to become the focal point for those who are monitoring the project. A completion date – which is set without adequate knowledge of problems and access to resources – becomes a nightmare for the project and damages both pleasure in the work and results. Essential quality requirements may be set aside in order to finish before the deadline.

We can take our point of departure in the milestone plan to illustrate how difficult it is to set a completion date. The plan shows that the project must go through a series of states. In order to reach a state, a range of activities which build upon each other must be carried out. In PSO projects many activities are processes for change in people and the organisation, which require maturation, understanding and support from members of the base organisation. In the early stages of a project the types of activity which must be performed later on are not known in detail. It is therefore a risky business to set a 100 per cent binding completion date. It will require large resources to work out a date which you are absolutely sure is achievable.

It is rather a matter of creating commitment between the principal parties. To the best of their ability and with a certain element of risk, they set completion dates.

Actually, a binding completion date can only be set if all activities to be performed, the people who will be included in the work, and all extraneous conditions which may affect the project, are known. In order to know all this, most of the work in the project must actually have been done. A feasibility study in which we roughly work our way through the central problems in the project is one method of obtaining a better basis for estimating the use of time and resources in the project. But even with such a basis it is difficult to work out a definite completion date.

Do not interpret what we have just said as meaning that we feel that there should be no time scheduling. Anticipated times for completion for respective milestones should be entered on the milestone plan. At the same time, it must be made very clear that these completion dates should be perceived as goals to work towards – not as absolutes to be used later to determine the success of the project.

In general we have recommended that a project be divided up into phases and sub-projects. The point of such a division is that we concentrate on one part of the project at a time, a part into which it is possible to have insight and which we can plan with a reasonable degree of certainty. Division into phases makes subsequent time planning more certain.

In order to be able to evaluate and set expected times for completion for the different milestones, we need:

❑ The milestone plan.

❑ An activity overview which supplements the milestone plan and which shows the most time- and resource-consuming activities.
❑ The project responsibility chart with agreed commitments on resources.

We have gone through the process of drawing up a milestone plan and a project responsibility chart. Time scheduling requires that we also prepare an overview of the most time- and resource-consuming activities which must be performed in order to reach the different milestones. The overview does not need to be complete; most important is that it include the activities which demand time and resources.

Time scheduling is performed in connection with the project responsibility chart. On the form (see Figure 5.9) there is a section for scheduling. This will be used now.

We take each milestone in turn. The work will be performed in three steps. First we pinpoint the activities which require a great deal of time and resources. Then we estimate the resource requirement for the milestone plan. The resource requirement can be stated in hours, days or weeks of work. Man days are usually used. Thereafter the calendar time is planned and the work is plotted on the time calendar.

Let us use the project 'Action plan for a better work environment' as an example. In Figure 5.12 we have shown the most time- and resource-consuming activities for the different milestones in this project. We can see that at this stage of planning we make certain decisions on how the milestones will be achieved. This is necessary to be able to draw up a time schedule. Among other things it is decided to send out a questionnaire to all employees to get inputs to the description of the present situation. It is also decided that line managers will be interviewed to provide a basis for drawing up a rough outline of the desired situation. Other measures with different resource and time requirements could have been chosen.

Using the milestone plan, project responsibility chart and the rough activity overview as a basis, we can start the scheduling. We look first at the work on the milestone which will end with a description of the present situation. Estimating the resources

M1 Description of present situation
- Prepare a questionnaire
- Wait for response
- Process the replies and collate them in a report

M2 Description of desired situation
- Interview line managers
- Prepare a proposal for the desired situation
- Decide on the desired situation

M3 Requirements for change
- Identify the most important requirements for change

M4 Ideas for measures
- Hold a brain-storming session

M5 Consequences of the measures
- Assess whether a measure will contribute towards the desired situation
- Calculate cost estimates for the measures

M6 Action plan
- Select the measures to be included in the plan
- Collate the measures in a plan
- Develop an action plan in detail

Figure 5.12 *Overview of the most time- and resource-comsuming activities in the project which will draw up an action plan to improve the work environment*

requirements for this milestone means assessing the work input required to reach it. We pose the question: If the work is performed in a concentrated manner, without any interruptions, how many days (or hours or weeks) of work will it take? The anticipated work input should be entered in the left-hand column of the responsibility chart.

In order to provide such an estimate we must look more closely at the resource-consuming activities involved in reaching the milestone. In this case the major part of the resources will be used in drawing up the questionnaire, processing the replies and drawing up the report. We know from the responsibility chart that the work will be a cooperative effort involving the project manager, the personnel consultant and the environment committee. The affected line managers must be consulted. The external consultant should provide assistance for training. These are the resources we assess for the work to be executed. We believe that the work will require ten man days.

Thereafter the work towards achieving the milestone should be put into calendar time. How long the work will take, and when it should be performed, depends on the availability of the people being considered and how time-consuming the different activities are. We know that in this case it is necessary to wait for a response to the questionnaire. This is not a resource-consuming activity, but it demands calendar time. Moreover, holidays, illness and other absences, interruptions and breaks in the work, and other tasks which project members will perform, must be taken into consideration. We calculate that it will take 20 calendar days to reach the milestone.

The time schedule for the milestone will be recorded on the form for the project responsibility chart; see Figure 5.13. The planned time period for working on the milestone will be marked with a horizontal line. The date set for completion can be marked with a vertical line.

We then proceed to the next milestone. We have shown that the work on developing a description of the desired situation will require 15 man days. The work on this milestone can start before the previous one is reached. Interviews with line managers can be prepared and dates can be agreed upon when there is a rough idea of the employees' picture of the present situation – there is no need to wait until the report is completed. When assessing how long work on this milestone will take, it is important to take the fact into consideration that this includes a decision-making process. Line managers and the managing director must decide how they want the work environment to be. It often takes longer to make these decisions than initially antic-ipated. It is important to form a clear picture of the time the decision-makers will need to arrive at their conclusions. Work on this milestone will take one month altogether.

Work on the next milestone follows the same procedure. Any feasibility or follow-up work can be marked with a dotted line on the time schedule. Some preparations for the writing of the action plan will be done at an early stage. This means that principles can be drawn up for the word-processed text, for example, and for the layout of the report. Special events, for example a seminar or, in this case, a brain-storming session, can be marked with an X.

The combination of a responsibility chart and a time schedule provides a good, focused picture of the planned progress of a project. When a schedule has been drawn up on the responsibility chart, the anticipated completion dates for the milestones can be transferred over to the milestone plan. We thus obtain a milestone plan with completion dates for the different milestones.

Figure 5.14 shows the milestone plan with completion dates for the 'work environment project'.

We again stress that we are talking about anticipated dates. Setting the completion date of the project is not the most important goal of project planning. Project planning should ensure first and foremost that the project works on the right things and that it has a good basis for achieving the desired end state.

Let us return to the situation where a project's date of completion is determined by conditions beyond the project's control. Outside forces (public authorities, a special event on a set date, a demanding customer) have determined that the results of the project must be available on a specific day. For example, the May 17th committee (responsible for preparing for the celebration of the Norwegian National Holiday) should be ready with its work by May 17th.

In such cases it is also relevant to perform the type of planning we have just demonstrated, but a problem may arise. If the imposed completion date really is an absolute requirement, and if it appears that the calculated project completion date is further in the future than this imposed date, the project faces a serious challenge.

In such cases it is important to hold a thorough and sober discussion about alternatives, either for an increased input of resources or for a reduced level of ambition, so that the project can be implemented within the time limit. Is it possible, perhaps, to find an acceptable combination of a slightly reduced level of ambition and a slightly increased input of resources? The work

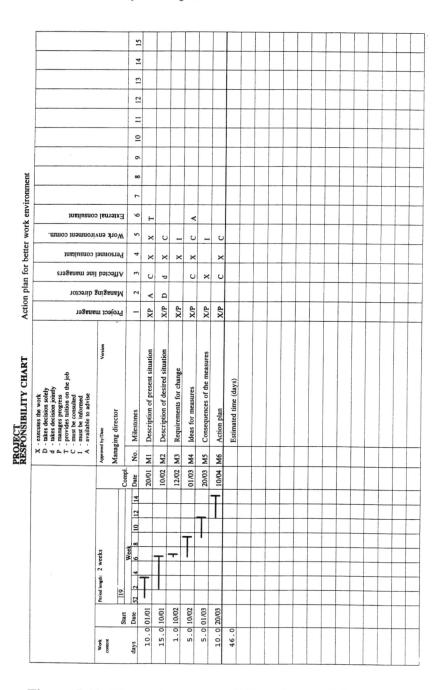

Figure 5.13 *The project responsibility chart and the activity schedule for the project which will draw up an action plan to improve the work environment*

MILESTONE PLAN   Action plan for better work environment

Planned date		Milestone description	Approved by/Date Managing director Project Manager	Version
		Project description	Date Report	
20/01	M1	When there is a description of the present situation		
10/02	M2	When there is a description of the desired situation		
12/02	M3	When the requirements for change are stated and prioritised		
01/03	M4	When ideas for measures to tackle the prioritised requirements for change are available		
20/03	M5	When an evaluation of the consequences of the various measures is available		
10/04	M6	When the selected measures are included in an action plan, which is submitted to the managing director		

Figure 5.14 *The milestone plan with completion dates for the milestones for the project which will draw up an action plan to improve the work environment*

on each milestone can be re-examined with a view to possible time-saving.

If it is not possible to find a solution which gives a completion date before the deadline, the problem must be dealt with by the proposer of the project or the organisation's management. An acceptable solution will then hopefully be found. If not – and the project still has a task which it cannot manage before the deadline – the project manager must consider seriously whether he is willing to accept the position of project manager and be responsible for a task where he is doomed to failure.

We will illustrate time planning with one more example. Figure 5.15 shows the completed time schedule for the project 'New premises for service, efficiency, job satisfaction and growth'.

On the time schedule a rough estimate has been made of the resources needed to reach the different milestones. Arriving at realistic estimates is often the most difficult part of working out a project responsibility chart. In the first stage it is the work input, not the time lapse, which should be estimated.

We will comment on some of the estimates in more detail to show the reasoning process.

CS1 Objective breakdown structure

The management group (managing director, head of finance, head of personnel, head of marketing) and in addition the project manager and project members from customer services/operations (4 people), 9 people altogether, will participate in a two-day development process. Thus there is a need for 18 man days. The consultant is not included in the calculation; his relevant time input and cost must be negotiated.

EC1 Work processes and improvement potential

The work consists of charting existing processes, establishing new ones, and identifying the efficiency potential. We have determined that there are 10 processes which must be described and

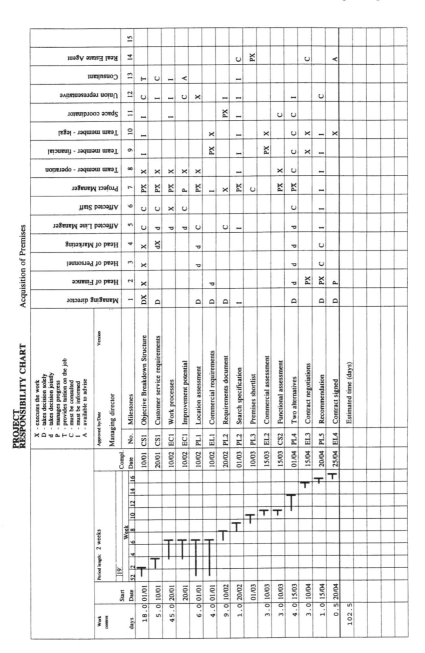

Figure 5.15 *Project responsibility chart and the activity schedule for the sub-project 'New premises for service, efficiency, job satisfaction and growth'*

evaluated. Each requires a total of $1\frac{1}{2}$ days and will be dealt with by a working group of an average of 3 people (different people are included in different groups). This means 10 processes $\times$ $1\frac{1}{2}$ days $\times$ 3 people $= 45$ man days.

PL2 Requirements document

The project manager will use 1 man day and the space coordinator 8 man days, which means 9 man days altogether.

EL2 Commercial assessment

The economist will use 2 man days and the lawyer 1 man day which makes 3 man days altogether.

In the resources column we can state the total resource requirement. We could have shown the calculations to make it easier to understand and remember the reasoning behind the resource estimates.

In this project several of the project members will be included in several different project tasks. In such cases it may be necessary to draw up a workload overview for each individual member to see whether they will be able to make the desired effort. In this overview, the whole range of tasks people have (not just implementation tasks, but also decisions and consultations, etc) must be taken into consideration.

It is necessary to look closely at the demands on the decision-makers. Will they have the time and opportunity to make the necessary decisions? We can mark milestones that require decisions with a vertical line on the time line indicating when the decision-making process should start.

After estimating the resource input, the work on the milestones will be put into calendar time. We can see from the figure that part of April is taken up with the Easter holiday and will not be used for project work. The dotted lines for individual milestones indicate that certain feasibility work should be completed before the actual work starts.

It is important not to draw up shorter deadlines than are necessary. For both PL1 and EL2 ample time is allowed for decision making.

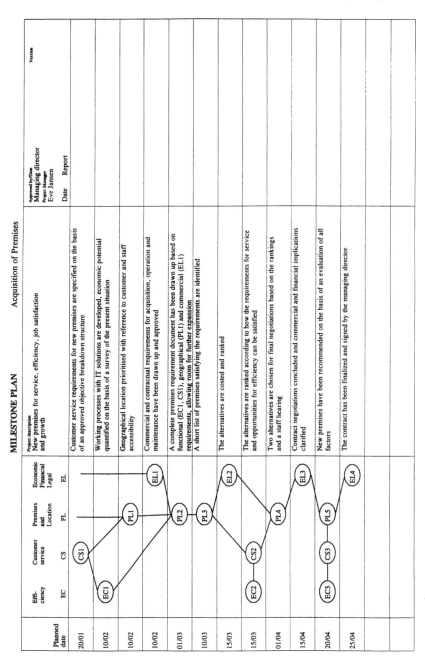

Figure 5.16 *The milestone plan with completion dates for the milestones for the sub-project 'New premises for service, efficiency, job satisfaction and growth'*

The activity schedule shows when the milestones are expected to be reached. Anticipated completion dates can be entered on the milestone plan. Figure 5.16 shows the milestone plan for the sub-project (shown earlier as Figure 4.11) supplemented with the planned completion dates for the milestones.

6

Detail Planning and Detail Organisation

In this chapter we will discuss detail planning and detail organisation. We deal with planning and organisation together on this level. We use the generic term *activity planning* for these two tasks.

We first present factors which are essential to pay heed to during activity planning. Thereafter we examine the approach to this type of planning. The activity responsibility chart plays a central role in activity planning.

PRINCIPLES OF ACTIVITY PLANNING

The first principle we emphasise is that planning and organisation of individual activities in a project should not be done before it is needed. One sees projects where detail plans are made for activities that will first be performed far in the future, in several months or years. It is very probable that this work is wasted. Before the day comes when the work should have started, changes will have occurred which render the plan useless.

It may even be that some planned activities will be dropped. The project has taken a course which makes them superfluous. And if they are to be executed, rational planning and organisation require that we know the foundation they will build on, the results of earlier tasks. We must also know which people will execute the work. Information of this type is not usually available before we are relatively close to the starting time for the activity.

The other principle we emphasise is that those who will perform the work must also be included in planning and organising it. This was also shown in Figure 5.11 (the example of a principle responsibility chart), which illustrated what is generally considered to be a good distribution of work between the line manager, project manager and implementors. When implementors participate in activity planning we make better plans and it leads to increased motivation and identification with the project. It produces better results.

Activity planning may well occur at normal project meetings, where reports on earlier activities in the project are examined, discussions on how to make up any delays are held, and general problems in the project are taken up.

ACTIVITY PLANNING

Activity planning is the drawing up of a plan to achieve the goals of the milestone plan. It is through activity planning that we work out how to reach the milestones within the time limits and with the resources allocated.

Activity responsibility chart

A major part of activity planning will be performed with the help of the activity responsibility chart. Therefore we will first examine what an activity responsibility chart is.

In the previous chapter we gave a general description of a responsibility chart. We also showed the use of the project responsibility chart, which clarifies the role of the different parties in achieving milestones. The activity responsibility chart is subordinate to the project responsibility chart. It will describe which people will perform the various activities, but the distribution of the work described must lie within the agreed guidelines on the project responsibility chart.

When making an activity responsibility chart we take the activities to be executed as the starting point. Then we decide which people should be linked to these activities. The project responsibility chart shows which parties the people should be drawn from.

The chart also describes who will have the right to make decisions or to express opinions.

The activity responsibility chart has one advantage in comparison with a number of other activity planning techniques, in that it not only shows who will perform the different activities, but it also brings attention to other important matters, such as decision-making authority, progress responsibility, consultation and information activities.

Making the activity responsibility chart is – in the same way as the work on the project responsibility chart was – an important clarification process. Those who will work on the activities must meet, discuss and arrive at an agreement on what the activity responsibility chart shall look like. Every person who is to have a role in the project must participate in this process and have the opportunity to apply the appropriate symbols to his own name.

It may be that when setting up a responsibility chart, certain individuals are allocated too many symbols. Some take too many jobs and roles upon themselves. Here the project manager must be on guard – overloaded project members can have a negative effect on the progress of the project. A 'crossing-off round' is sometimes necessary.

Some people will want to take on jobs for which they have neither the expertise nor the authority. The activity responsibility chart makes it possible to establish the principle that professional decisions should be made by those who are normally responsible for them in the base organisation. These are the people who should be linked to the decision-making symbol. And an important point – it is only those people who actually have a decision-making symbol on the responsibility chart who should make decisions. There is a strong tendency in projects for everyone to want to join in and discuss everything – including matters for which they are not responsible and do not have the expertise. This hinders the project. This type of over-enthusiasm can be prevented if the activity responsibility chart is set up properly and followed.

The activity responsibility chart organises work on the activities in the project. In order for it to be a plan to work to, we need to supplement the activity responsibility chart with a time schedule. Estimates for the use of resources must be made and the work on the different activities must be put into calendar time.

The activity responsibility chart does not need to repeat the responsibility for decision-making processes if they are described precisely enough on the project responsibility chart. Decision symbols on the activity responsibility chart often stand for quality approval.

Stages in activity planning

We 'activity plan' each milestone individually. We do not start activity planning before it is necessary. The person who is responsible for progress for the milestone (capital letter 'P' on the project responsibility chart) must, together with the project manager, decide when the planning work should start. Activity planning can be divided into four stages:

1. Identify all the activities that must be performed to reach the milestone.
2. Identify all the people who will be affected by each activity, and determine in which way they should be involved in the work on it.
3. Estimate the work input necessary for the execution of each activity.
4. Put the work on each activity into calendar time.

It is usual for planning to take place at a project meeting where all the affected project members are present.

Stage 1

It is best to draw up an individual activity plan for each milestone. The first stage in the work will thus be to find all the activities that must be completed to reach the first milestone. A great deal of help is provided here by the work done in connection with time scheduling for the milestone plan. This provides a starting point for activity planning but the final list of activities may be completely different from the one set up in connection with the milestone plan.

There are several reasons for this, among others that:

- The list of activities previously developed was not intended to be complete.
- A great deal of guesswork lay behind the initial list.
- The activities already completed in the project have raised the level of knowledge of what should now be done.
- A completely different approach from that originally considered can be chosen.
- The level of ambition may have changed significantly.

The list of activities worked out doing time scheduling is a good basis for the work on finding relevant activities now. Further support can be obtained if there is a model to show how this work should be executed. (For example, a systems development model may be of assistance if a computer system is to be developed.) We speak more of this later.

An activity should fulfil certain requirements:

- It should not require an unduly large work input – a maximum of 80 man hours or 10 man days.
- It must be possible to check that the activity has been completed.

Both requirements facilitate control. If an activity is very large regarding work input and calendar time, it is difficult to do the controlling job. The reports may for a long time say that everything is going well, and suddenly – the day the activity should be completed, problems arise. The activity is by no means finished, and a considerable amount of work remains. This may also occur with smaller activities, but the point is that here it can be detected much more quickly if the work is not going as planned.

It is also important that it is possible to ascertain whether the activity has been finished and it may be necessary to set up specific criteria to ensure that this is so. One alternative is that a person other than the implementor must state whether the activity has been carried out satisfactorily. If there are no criteria which make it possible to check whether the activity is completed and maintains standards of quality, it is difficult to control.

Stage 2

The people to be involved in the work must be determined for each individual activity. In this we are assisted by the project responsibility chart, which establishes which parties should be included in realising the particular milestones. The base organisation will already have approved its contents. The symbols representing the roles are placed in the body of the responsibility matrix.

Stage 3

When it is decided who should perform an activity and roles have been established, the amount of resources required to carry out the plan must be estimated. Work content will be stated in man hours, days or weeks.

The project manager and the implementor(s) jointly decide on the extent of resources required. As indicated previously, it is very important that this occur through cooperation between the two parties.

After stage 2, a copy of the responsibility chart is usually given to each participant. Individuals estimate their resource requirements on their own copy. This can be done by individual completion of the left-hand (estimate) column, or the implementors can replace the 'X's on the responsibility chart with their estimates for resource requirement. Next, the estimates will be discussed with the project manager.

Stage 4

When the amount of work input required for implementation of the activity is established, we discuss how it should be laid out in calendar time. During this assessment the activities which precede and immediately follow should be taken into consideration.

The project manager must decide when it is best to carry out the activity. However, if the implementor is in the base organisation, the line manager (who is the person who can commit the use of resources) and the implementor should be brought into the discussion as to when the activity can actually be implemented. There may be factors in the base organisation which mean that the activity must be scheduled for another time, even when this is not ideal seen from the project's point of view.

When assigning an activity to calendar time, the fact that a member seldom spends 100 per cent of his time on the project must be taken into consideration. In addition to the project member's other duties, factors such as illness, compassionate leave, courses and seminars, etc must be considered.

Through scheduling, an understanding of which activities are time-critical is gained. These are the activities which are such that if they are delayed, the whole project is delayed. At a project meeting it may be relevant to discuss the allocation of jobs so that the activities which will be time-critical are also the ones over which one has most control.

The responsibility for time-critical activities should not lie with those who have a very heavy workload, either within the project or outside it. In order to avoid this, jobs and responsibilities can be redistributed or relief arrangements set up. This should also be discussed at the project meeting.

Figure 6.1 shows an example of an activity responsibility chart. This is the 'work environment project' which has now progressed so far that the activities leading up to the first milestone M1 'When there is a description of the present situation' have been identified. It is now important that the activity list is complete. It is no longer sufficient to indicate simply the most time- and resource-consuming activities as we did in the time scheduling in Figure 5.12.

Tools in activity planning

We recommend that support in the form of previous experience and other relevant material be sought in activity planning. At this level of planning, thoroughness and precision are more important than creativity.

It may be an advantage to have a general model for the actual work to act as a guideline. A model which states which activities must be executed is helpful, as it can ensure that no activities will be forgotten. It is obviously an advantage to have a model which has a direct connection with the type of problem

ACTIVITY SCHEDULE

Action plan for better work environment

M1 — When there is a description of the present situation

Period length: 1 week

Legend:
- X - executes the work
- D - takes decision solely
- d - takes decision jointly
- P - manages progress
- T - provides tuition on the job
- C - must be consulted
- I - must be informed
- A - available to advise

No.	Activities	Compl. Date	Work content (days)	Start Date	Karyn - project manager (1)	Alan - managing director (2)	Mary - head production (3)	Paul - head sales (4)	Louise - head personnel (5)	Barry - personnel cons. (6)	Rose - Work Env. Comm. (7)	Arnold - consultant (8)
1	Draw up draft of a questionnaire	06/01	4.0	04/01	X/P					X		
2	Gather views on the questionnaire	10/01	1.0	08/01	P	A	C	C	C			
3	Determine final form questionnaire	11/01	1.0	09/01	X/P					X		T
4	Set up mailing list	10/01	1.0	04/01						X/P		
5	Send out the questionnaire	12/01	0.5	12/01						X/P		
6	Send out reminders	17/01	0.5	17/01	X/P					X/P		
7	Process the replies	19/01	2.0	12/01	X/P					X		A
8	Draw up the report	20/01	3.0	16/01	X/P					X		A
	Estimated time (days)		13.0									

Figure 6.1 *The activity responsibility chart for the first milestone of the project which will draw up an action plan to improve the work environment*

the project is working on. For a PSO project we should consequently have a model which is relevant to this type of work.

Since each project is unique, it may be difficult to find
models which are directly relevant to our particular problem. A
general problem-solving model, a general description of how to
proceed to solve a problem, may then be useful.

Example of an activity responsibility chart

Returning to our relocation example, let us take another look at
the sub-project 'New premises for service, efficiency, job satisfaction and growth'. We will examine the activity planning for
one milestone. We have chosen milestone EC1 'Work processes
for IT solutions developed, profit potential quantified on the
basis of a survey of the present situation'.

This is an important milestone. The project is indeed intended
to lead to improved customer service and greater efficiency in
the new premises. For these to be more than just fine words, the
project is obliged to describe existing work processes in order to
obtain a picture of the present situation. When this is obtained, a
discussion must follow about what can be done better in the new
premises with the integration of the previously dispersed business. Finally, desired future work processes for the new
premises must be described. The gains to be made by working
in the new and improved way should also be indicated.

Figure 6.2 shows the activity responsibility chart for milestone EC1.

The project chooses to describe the present processes with the
help of wall charts. This is a technique where a business process
is given a large-size description using actual documents to show
explicitly what is going on. The project requires an external
consultant to assist in this work. A clearance signal for this was
given on the project responsibility chart.

After the processes have been described, one day is set aside
for a joint discussion in order to obtain a complete overview and
to discuss the new solutions and processes. The work will
conclude by identifying the potential for gains. When evaluating
the gains, we look at opportunities for saving resources, reducing

ACTIVITY SCHEDULE — Acquisition of Premises

EC1
Working processes with IT solutions are developed, economic potential quantified on the basis of a survey of the present situation

Period length: 1 week

Legend:
- X - executes the work
- D - takes decision solely
- d - takes decision jointly
- P - manages progress
- T - provides tuition on the job
- C - must be consulted
- I - must be informed
- A - available to advise

No.	Activities	Work content (days)	Start Date	Compl. Date	Eve (project manager) 1	Paul (sales) 2	Arthur (orders) 3	Kerstin (accounts) 4	Oscar (warehouses) 5	Thor (service) 6	Joe (purchasing) 7	William (IT) 8	Brigitte (employee rep) 9	Tom (consultant) 10
1	Map work processes sales	14.0	20/01	25/01	X	X/P	X	X	X			I		T
2	Map work processes purchasing	4.0	25/01	28/01	X		X	X	X	X	X/P	I		T
3	Map work processes service	4.0	25/01	28/01	X	X			X	X/P	X	I		T
4	Map work processes accounts	2.0	28/01	30/01	X/P			X/P				I		T
5	Plan "discussion" day	2.0	01/02	03/02	X/P	X	X	X	X	X	X	X	X	X
6	"Discussion" day	9.0	05/02	05/02	C	X/P	X	C	C			X	X	X
7	Document new processes sales	2.0	06/02	08/02	C	C		C	C		X/P	C		A
8	Document new processes purchasing	1.0	06/02	08/02	C					X/P		C		A
9	Document new processes service	1.0	06/02	08/02	C			X/P		X/P		C		A
10	Document new processes accounts	1.0	06/02	08/02	C	X	X	X	X	X	X	C		A
11	Calculate potential for gains	6.0	09/02	10/02	X/P	X	X	X	X				C	
	Estimated time (days)	46.0			9.0	6.5	6.0	7.0	6.0	4.5	4.0	2.0	1.0	

Week: 3 4 5 6 ... (19)

Figure 6.2 *The activity responsibility chart for the milestone EC1 of the sub-project 'New premises for service, efficiency, job satisfaction and growth'*

stock and wastage, and also what will be gained through improvements in quality which lead to more satisfied customers and greater sales.

The responsibility chart in Figure 6.2 shows the distribution of roles with the use of letters. The project has also drawn up a responsibility chart where the 'X's are replaced with estimates in man days. This is shown in Figure 6.3. From this we can see that Eve must spend 9 man days on the different activities in connection with milestone EC1. The whole should occur over the course of 3 weeks, that is to say 15 man days. Others will participate with 6–7 man days in the same period. This means that Eve and the others must obtain genuine release and cover for their daily jobs if the responsibility chart is to be valid.

ACTIVITY SCHEDULE — Acquisition of Premises

EC1

Working processes with IT solutions are developed, economic potential quantified on the basis of a survey of the present situation

Period length: 1 week — Start 20/01 — Week 19?

Legend:
- X - executes the work
- D - takes decision solely
- d - takes decision jointly
- P - manages progress
- T - provides tuition on the job
- C - must be consulted
- I - must be informed
- A - available to advise

No.	Activities	Work content (days)	Start Date	Compl. Date	Eve (project manager) 1	Paul (sales) 2	Arthur (orders) 3	Kerstin (accounts) 4	Oscar (warehouses) 5	Thor (service) 6	Joe (purchasing) 7	William (IT) 8	Brigitte (employee rep) 9	Tom (consultant) 10
1	Map work processes sales	14.0	20/01	25/01	2.0	3.0	3.0	3.0	3.0					
2	Map work processes purchasing	4.0	25/01	28/01	0.5	1.0	0.5	0.5	1.0	1.0	1.0			
3	Map work processes service	4.0	25/01	28/01	0.5		0.5		0.5	1.0	0.5			
4	Map work processes accounts	2.0	28/01	30/01	1.0			1.0						
5	Plan "discussion" day	2.0	01/02	03/02	1.0									
6	"Discussion" day	9.0	05/02	05/02	1.0	1.0	1.0	1.0	1.0	1.0	1.0	1.0	1.0	
7	Document new processes sales	2.0	06/02	08/02		1.0	1.0					1.0		
8	Document new processes purchasing	1.0	06/02	08/02							1.0			
9	Document new processes service	1.0	06/02	08/02						1.0				
10	Document new processes accounts	1.0	06/02	08/02				1.0						
11	Calculate potential for gains	6.0	09/02	10/02	3.0	0.5	0.5	0.5	0.5	0.5	0.5	2.0	1.0	
	Estimated time (days)	46.0			9.0	6.5	6.0	7.0	6.0	4.5	4.0	2.0		

Figure 6.3 *A supplementary activity responsibility chart for the milestone EC1 of the sub-project 'New premises for service, efficiency, job satisfaction and growth'*

7

Project Control

WHAT IS CONTROL?

Many people believe that monitoring and project control are one and the same thing. This is not so. Reporting is describing what has occurred and what the situation is. Control is doing something about what the reports show.

We must have reports to be able to check whether the project is sticking to the plan. The purpose of reports is not to establish grounds for punishment or reward. The purpose is to establish whether there is a need for corrective measures – while there is still time to take those measures.

Control is management, not paperwork. Control involves analysing the situation, deciding what to do and doing it. But control presupposes that a certain amount of paperwork (reporting) be done.

Control is the crux of project management. Nevertheless, it is often misunderstood both by management and project staff. The reason may be that people have had many negative experiences. They are used to extensive bureaucracy, where reports are sent out left, right and centre, while everyone knows that, at best, no one reads them, or in the worst case they are used to denounce those who are not following the plan.

Control is *not* the same as persecution. Reports are needed not to find out whether people have been on the job eight hours a day, but to determine whether or not it is necessary to change course. Project management must have the ability to make decisions based on the reports they receive, otherwise all reporting is in vain.

Let us illustrate what control is by looking at decisions that can be made if reporting reveals that there is a lapse in project progress. When it shows that it is not possible to achieve the completion date set for an activity or a milestone, the following possibilities exist:

❑ move the milestone date;
❑ lower the level of ambition;
❑ bring in additional resources;
❑ rearrange the workload.

One may accept the consequences of being delayed by deciding to move the current milestone and any subsequent milestone. If one does not wish to do this, the deadline can be met if the level of ambition is lowered. This is not always feasible but often it will be possible to do something. One may in addition bring in more, or more competent, resources. Again we know that it is difficult in practice to achieve great effects through increased resources, but it may be possible to get some benefit. Work can also be redistributed, for example, assigning the most able people to the most time-critical activities.

Not everyone believes that it helps to bring additional resources into projects. Brooks coined his law on the basis of his experiences when working on the operating system for the IBM 360 series. It states: 'Adding resources to a late project makes it later.' Brooks had delayed software projects in mind when he formulated this law, but today it is used for all types of projects. The background for it is that when staffing is increased in a project, those who are already working on it have to spend time introducing the new staff to the project and training them. Real work input into the project's activities actually falls.

Our basic point is that there are two attitudes which are not permitted and which damage all project work. They are:

❑ 'It will probably be OK.'
❑ 'We'll wait and see.'

We warn against a 'head-in-the-sand' mentality, where people are not willing to acknowledge problems and initiate the necessary measures.

It is not a good thing if a plan is off schedule and nobody realises it before it is too late to do anything about it. But as a rule this is not the main problem. The most common problem is that people know that a plan is off schedule, but they do not have the will or the power to do anything about it.

Below we present certain principles and tools that can strengthen control of project work.

PRINCIPLES OF CONTROL

We will first formulate certain principles that we consider to be fundamental for reporting and control. Thereafter we will show how they can be used in practice.

Good reporting

In the majority of cases reporting is tedious. This applies especially when things are going badly. It is not pleasant to report that the project is not going according to plan.

Exception reporting is a much used reporting principle. It means that only variances from the plan will be reported (and these are mainly negative variances). We are opposed to this. It means that people can only communicate when there are problems, and this is not particularly pleasant, either for the person receiving or the person providing the information. A communication imbalance is formed in the organisation – a preoccupation with everything that goes wrong. It is also important to bring out what is going according to plan.

Even if everything is going well, however, reporting is often perceived to be bureaucratic and tedious. It is associated with 'desk work' which takes time away from what should actually be done. This perception will never be eradicated completely, but it can be minimised. In practice, this means reporting should be reduced to the absolute minimum with regard to control. It also means that a balance must be found between written reporting (which is particularly tedious) and conversations and group discussions which elaborate on matters raised in the report wherever necessary.

Something that creates a particular distaste for reporting is the feeling that the whole reporting process is worthless because it is done as a matter of habit rather than as a basis for action. It is done because it is an accepted required procedure, but without enthusiasm and without any belief that it will improve the work situation for oneself or for the project.

Many people have filled in large report forms, and seen them collected, sorted and put in a file on a shelf. The project manager is often unwilling to go into issues discussed in the report. The most that comes of these issues is that he will 'make a note of them'. Project members know that the only thing the project manager is concerned about is that everyone has submitted his report.

This attitude can be changed if project members feel that control is actually taking place. It must happen through discussions and analysis, and result in measures which improve the situation for the project. Then reporting will be experienced as being useful and motivating.

Defining the criteria before work begins

Effective control requires that you decide in advance which matters must be kept under special review during the project. Matters to be reported on and discussed must have been identified when control measures are established. If project members are allowed to report on what they consider to be most important, haphazard reporting will result. Clearly defined control criteria should exist and be built into the report form.

We should not allow reporting from project members to depend too much on free text. The result tends to be very short messages ('OK') or long accounts of trivialities. There is a danger the report will reflect the temporary energy level of the report writer (which can be low on a Friday afternoon) or his linguistic ability to camouflage the real state of affairs.

We recommend that one focuses instead on some previously defined conditions. It is important to make reporting so simple that the words 'Yes' and 'No' are sufficient. If it is necessary to elaborate further on matters, do so in a conversation.

Conversations held as a link in reporting and control must be structured. Many conversations between the project manager and project members are not really goal-directed and mostly take the form of a 'cosy chat'. The project manager perches on the edge of the member's desk and asks 'How's it going?' The conversation ranges back and forth over more or less chance matters in the project.

The report form should, as mentioned, focus on previously defined control criteria. It is just as important that any supplementary conversations also have the same focus. Conversations must be directed towards discovering the causes of any deficiencies and identify action to put the project back on course.

We also stress that it is important that the reporting and control discussions occur between the people who are responsible for these tasks, as shown by the principle responsibility chart. In practice we often see that status reports and discussions occur at project meetings where a range of people are present who have no or only a peripheral connection with the matter in hand. The presence of these people hampers the openness necessary for discussion of an unpleasant situation and the possible choice of unpopular measures. They rarely have anything to contribute to the discussion and in the best case only serve to prolong it.

Reporting on the plans

It is an important principle that reporting should occur on a document which also shows the actual plan. Each time a report is made, it must subsequently be compared with the plan. This ensures that one keeps to the point. Other reporting methods should not be permitted.

In order to simplify reporting, the plan document should be drawn up in such a way that there is room for it. When the plan is finalised, sufficient copies should be prepared for use during all subsequent reporting.

Reporting on the plan document also has the advantage that we can see more easily that the right person receives reports and follows up. It is important to send a report which shows a deviation from the plan to the person who has the authority to do something about the plan, or who can take steps to get on course again.

Reporting according to a predetermined pattern

All reporting should be done according to a set pattern. This often means that reports will be given at fixed intervals. Discipline is necessary otherwise it is easy for reporting to be neglected.

The frequency of reporting depends on the level. Reports can be less frequent at the milestone level than at the detail level because of the longer time horizon. It is more important that variances be detected quickly at detail level so that corrective measures can be introduced before these variances have gone on too long.

In general we recommend monthly reporting and control at the milestone plan level. Alternatively we can follow the principle that there should be a report each time a milestone is scheduled to be reached. At the activity level the frequency of reporting must be agreed upon internally within the project. Usually reporting every 14 days is appropriate.

CONTROLLING ACTIVITIES

We will begin by discussing control of activities. It is natural to start there, as it is what is going on at this level which governs what must be done at the milestone level.

Criteria for controlling activities

Activity plans will be drawn up and documented on the responsibility chart form. In accordance with the control principles, reporting will occur on the plan document. Figure 5.9 showed the responsibility chart form. We will now look more closely at the report section.

The form asks for reporting on seven different matters:

1. Use of resources.
2. Time schedule.
3. Quality.
4. Responsibility chart.
5. Changes/additions.

6. Waiting time.
7. Special problems.

Use of resources

The use of resources in the project is obviously one of the matters which must be monitored. It is important to ascertain whether one has used, or will use, the resources stated in the plan. We recommend reports on:

❏ actual resources used to the present;
❏ outstanding requirement for resources.

A simple summary can then be drawn up and compared with the estimate, to monitor the overall usage of resources. Our experience is that it is easier to get a project member to give a good estimate of the outstanding requirement than to ask him to give a percentage estimate of the completion status. When asked for a percentage figure, it is tempting to say that the activity is 90 per cent complete even if it hasn't progressed nearly so far.

On the report form there is a question on 'Work done' and 'Work to do'. It is answered by stating the respective actual use of resources until then and future needs for resources in the same unit (man hours, days or weeks) as was used for the estimate in the plan. If the activity has been completed, 0 is written under 'Work to do'.

Time schedule

The question of whether the project is on schedule, ie whether the activity will be completed on time, is also important. The plan shows when the activity should be completed. In the report we could pose the question: Completed on time? The question must be answered Yes or No. As an alternative we could ask for the completion date.

Quality

Over the last few years there has been increased attention to the importance of quality. It is important to be sure that this philosophy also reigns in project work.

One of the most frequent causes of delays in projects is that the original quality of the work is not good enough. Work may have been executed inaccurately or incompletely, so that it has to be repeated. This is therefore grounds for asking for a report on whether the quality is approved. Quality approval can be agreed upon, but is often one of the things that is neglected in practice. Therefore the question: Is quality accepted? must be answered Yes or No.

Responsibility chart

The responsibility chart defines precisely who should perform the various roles in connection with an activity. Experience has shown that there can be problems releasing the necessary people from their daily jobs in the base organisation. In projects it can also be difficult to achieve the necessary decisions. It is therefore important to have a report on whether the work pattern described by the responsibility chart is essentially being followed, or whether there are any variances. The form asks: Is the responsibility chart kept? The question must be answered Yes or No.

Changes/additions

It is important to ascertain whether the plan in its original form is being used as the basis for the work. It is often the case that when starting to work on an activity, new information comes to light and it becomes obvious that things should be done differently. When evaluating the use of resources and project progress, one needs to know whether the work was done according to the original plan, or whether changes or additions were introduced. Therefore the question: Changes required? must be answered Yes or No.

Waiting time

A project works with limited resources. It is therefore important to use the available resources in the best possible way. If someone is sitting around with nothing to do, this is a waste of resources and should be avoided. Therefore we ask the question: Waiting time? The question must be answered Yes or No.

Special problems

It is also desirable to know whether there have been any special problems along the way. It is not always easy for the project manager to detect all the problems. Therefore the report writer is given an opportunity to indicate whether he has experienced any difficulties. He is asked the question: Special problems? It must be answered Yes or No.

In addition, the report section offers an opportunity to elaborate on what seems to be the central problem in the project. We are given an opportunity to specify:

❑ problem description;
❑ cause: why the problem has arisen;
❑ consequence: what the consequences of the problem are for the project;
❑ suggested action: what can be done about the problem.

The form allows the report writer to indicate whether the variances from the plan or the problems the person concerned has taken up are so serious that they will have implications at the milestone level. He should state whether what has been reported has any consequences for the milestone plan. This means that project members should look at their own work and that of the team with this question in mind, which gives them a valuable perspective on what they are doing and on the problems they may experience.

Our suggested basis for reporting is, in essence, some simple questions which can be answered yes or no, and an overview of actual and anticipated use of resources.

This type of reporting is not very onerous, yet provides the person responsible for control with a good basis for further work. We take it for granted that the report only provides a starting point for a dialogue, where there is a closer examination of what the real problems in the project are.

Report dialogue

The report should provide a point of departure for a deeper discussion between the project manager and the team. This is especially true if the use of resources is expected to deviate from that estimated, or if one or more unsatisfactory answers are discovered on the report. A discussion about the project situation motivates better reporting and improves the project environment. It shows that reporting and control are taken seriously.

The starting point for the discussion must be that it is not an irreversible tragedy if the plan has gone off course. It is much worse if the project manager does not realise the problematic situation in time.

The plan must not be allowed to become a tyrant. The members must not be so afraid of variances that they do not dare report them. But neither should it be the case that people just add 10 per cent if the plan is in trouble. The plan should be viewed as *binding*. Vigorous efforts should be made to discover what is going wrong.

Discussions between the project manager and project members must therefore be goal-directed. They must be clearly structured with regard to discovering the real causes for any deviation between the plan and the actual situation.

We will take up some factors which are important when discussing the different headings in the report.

Use of resources

If a resource estimate shows itself to be wrong, it is important to clarify whether this is a one-time error, or whether we are facing a systematic estimation error. Particularly when several similar examples of variance are discovered, it should lead us to believe there has been a general miscalculation. The consequence of this should be that the estimation methods should be re-examined and all the estimates reevaluated.

One cause of inaccurate resource estimates is often that the project members' expertise is overrated. People are asked to do work for which they are not qualified. Plans and estimates must be drawn up based on the people available – they must not be based on brilliant people who do not exist. If project members do not have the necessary knowledge at the outset, time for training must be built in to the plans at the start.

Time schedule

The time schedule can be adhered to even if the need for resources for an activity has been underestimated. This means that slack is built into the schedule. Again, it is important to discuss whether this is unique to the current situation, or a product of the general way of doing scheduling. If one has been generous when making the schedule, one knows that there is some leeway in the outstanding activities.

If the time schedule cannot hold, it is important first to clarify the implications of this for the project. If the activity which has been delayed is a critical activity, the whole project will be delayed unless measures are taken to make up for this lost time.

If the time schedule breaks down and it cannot be traced back to inadequate resource estimates, it is important to find the cause of the problem. There may be several other reasons for the inaccuracy. We will mention some typical causes.

- ❏ Unforeseen interruption in the work. Examples are illness, compassionate leave and strikes. These are matters that cannot be anticipated.
- ❏ No plans for releasing personnel from the base organisation who will participate in the project. This means that line management have not arranged cover so that the project members can participate to the extent planned.
- ❏ Deliberate downgrading of the project on the part of the line management. Matters may have arisen in the base organisation which justify this. Resources will then not be supplied to the project at the rate calculated during planning.
- ❏ Lower priority on the part of the project members. In such cases cover plans exist for the project members so that they do have the formal opportunity to participate in the project work as planned. Nevertheless, they regard the work in the base organisation as being more important (for example, because of poor motivation for the project or because they feel incompetent) and downgrade participation in the project.
- ❏ Poor project management. Cover plans exist, and the project members are willing to make an input, but poor project management might mean that the potential project members are not informed as to when they should participate.

This list illustrates that different problems require completely different solutions. Without knowing the actual causes for getting off schedule, it is not possible to work out the right corrective measures. We simply have to accept a deliberate downgrading by management (and revise plans accordingly), but something can be done about the lack of release plans or poor motivation.

In the matrix in Figure 7.1 we have shown certain combinations of possible answers to questions on whether the resource estimates and the schedule still hold. The matrix points out what it is particularly important to discuss.

		Time schedule accurate?	
		Yes	No
Work-content estimate accurate?	Yes	No action	Analyse - scheduling methods - cause of delay
	No	Analyse - estimating methods - cause of inaccuracy	Analyse - all four factors

Figure 7.1 *Analysing the accuracy of work content estimates and time schedules*

Quality

We have stressed earlier the importance of the quality of what is produced. On the reporting form we ask whether quality has been approved. Our experience is that one of the most important grounds for failure to complete the whole project within time and budget is that the work on earlier activities does not fulfil quality requirements. This has serious repercussions. Therefore quality must be regarded as just as important as keeping to schedule and everyone in the project must accept that quality will be evaluated. Responsibility for quality control can be decided through the principle responsibility chart and be put into concrete terms on the activity responsibility chart.

Quality control presupposes that people have agreed on what quality is, that the criteria for assessing the result have been decided. This is difficult, especially with PSO projects. In many cases the best method of ensuring quality is to select methods which one knows through experience will give good results.

We will discuss questions on quality in more detail in Chapter 8 and particularly in Chapter 9.

Responsibility chart

On the reporting form you will be asked whether the responsibility chart has been followed. For an ordinary project member it is the activity responsibility chart which is most relevant, and the answer will probably be based on it.

A 'No' to the question must be followed up with a more detailed discussion of the responsibility chart. The most common problem is that project members from the base organisation are not released to the extent required by the plan, but other problems may also exist.

Changes/additions

One heading on the reporting form asks whether any changes/additions have been made in relation to the plan. When planning occurs a relatively short time before the activity itself is to be performed, the need for changes is less than in cases where planning occurs a long time in advance. In any case, changes may occur. The most important reasons are:

❑ Changes occur in some of the underlying assumptions that the project is based on. These changes may be externally generated (the authorities have passed new regulations which affect whatever is to be done) or come from the base organisation (management have issued new guidelines).

❑ There is a flaw in the specifications of what the project should achieve. Detail work may reveal that there are flaws or omissions in the specifications upon which the project was based. This may lead to the product being somewhat different from what was originally intended.

❑ 'Eating whets the appetite'. It is very common for people to become more and more ambitious as work progresses well and for the scope of work to expand beyond what was originally foreseen.

We have to put up with changes, but they must be controllable. Uncontrolled changes are one of the important causes of project 'breakdown'. We simply have to accept certain changes (changes from outside or from the sponsor), but it is important to examine the consequences and revise plans.

Other types of changes must be subject to evaluation. Many good ideas crop up along the way in a project; they should not be accepted without being studied and their impact assessed. A formalised change procedure is necessary in a project. In order to be able to control a project it is important to have an overview of changes which occur.

Waiting time

Good utilisation of available resources in a project is important. It is sometimes necessary to transfer resources from one activity to another. We have available good computer programs which help us determine which activities are time-critical and what can be gained by transferring resources from one activity to another.

The project manager must perform this type of assessment, but it is important, particularly on motivational grounds, that he involve the project members in such discussions.

Example of an activity report

We are following the project 'New premises for service, efficiency, job satisfaction and growth'. Figure 7.2 is an example of an activity report. The report was issued on 10 February and applies to activities included in the work towards milestone EC1.

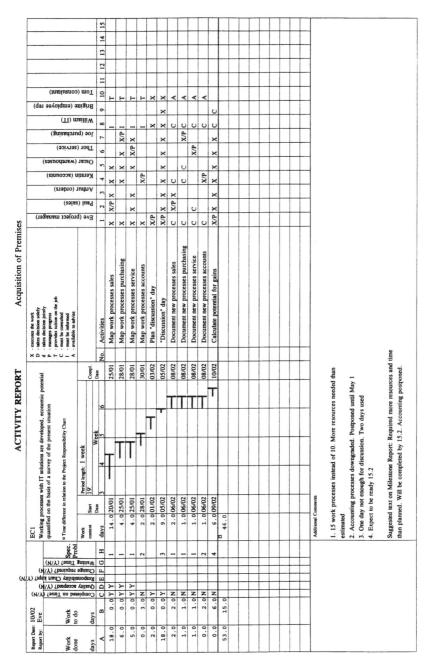

Figure 7.2 *Activity report for the milestone EC1 of the sub-project 'New premises for service, efficiency, job satisfaction and growth'*

The project has been postponed by an 'estimation failure'. The resources needed for describing and evaluating the work processes were underestimated. It is not that uncommon that a wrong assessment is made for such jobs. We can see that there were 15 processes instead of the 10 which were planned for. In addition, a one-day seminar took two days. This amounts to a lot of time when nine people are involved.

To get back on course, accounting processes have been downgraded and postponed. They are not that important at this point, because they have no significance either for the choice of the new premises or for the space programme.

CONTROLLING MILESTONES

Correlation between control at activity and milestone levels

We have seen how reporting at the activity level should be performed. The project members report using the form on which the activity plan (activity responsibility chart and time schedule) is described. The report shows clearly whether the plan is being followed. Discussions between the project manager and the project members elaborate on the causes of any discrepancy between the plan and the actual situation.

The project members also know the milestone plan. In their reports they will state whether unwanted developments at activity level have implications for the milestone plan.

The milestone plan is the project's global plan. It is the project manager's responsibility to report on how the project is developing in relation to the milestone plan. The reports are usually sent to the sponsor of the project (for example the managing director or a line manager) or to a steering committee. Others also receive the reports for information purposes. The principle responsibility chart shows who should receive the milestone reports.

It is the project manager's responsibility to follow up the activity reports from the project members. This means that the project manager must introduce corrective measures where needed. In certain cases it must be accepted that the plan can no longer be adhered to, and a revised plan must be developed.

Even if project members have stated that the situation at activity level has implications for the milestone plan, this may be avoided if adequate measures to correct the situation are introduced.

Criteria for controlling milestones

The project manager reports on the milestone plan. The report consists of two parts:

1. The milestones (which are also described verbally) and their mutual dependencies.
2. The expected completion dates for the milestones.

Reporting must cover both of these aspects.

The milestones

The milestones play a central role in project management. They express important states through which the project should pass. In a number of cases they also represent important results and have an intrinsic value beyond that of being checkpoints.

Reporting must give an account of which milestones have been reached. It should also state whether anything in particular has occurred in the work toward reaching the milestone which is of interest for the sponsor of the project or the steering committee.

Completion dates

We have discussed earlier the role played by the milestone completion dates and the project final date. We have said that in many cases factors other than these deadlines are of more importance. We have tried to tone down the focus on dates, but this does not mean that the set completion dates are not important. The project manager must then regard them as goals, and realise that the project will be assessed on whether or not it manages to stay on schedule.

It is therefore important to check the completion dates at the milestone level. Any variance from the anticipated completion date for a milestone must be reported. Equally important as reporting the variance is clarifying the causes for its occurrence.

Report dialogue

In principle, reports should be made on a form that also shows the plan. Obviously this also applies to milestone reports and there is room for this on the milestone form.

Reporting here is less structured than at the activity level. To a great extent, the project manager determines what to report. We assume that he has the ability to analyse the project situation and report the central issues. It is usual to mention the completion of important activities on the milestone plan.

The project manager must always report whether the completion dates for milestones are being adhered to. There is little room for an analysis of the problems on the form, so this must be done in a separate note when necessary. It may be wise not to circulate such an analysis to everyone interested in the progress of the project. It may indeed contain evaluations which, on personal or organisational grounds, should have limited distribution.

The milestone report should be a concise account from the project manager to the project sponsor, steering committee and key people in the base organisation. The idea is not that they should have a great deal to read but that they should be able to see at a glance where the project stands. If there are serious problems, they require elaboration in the form of memos and discussions.

If progress has slowed down in relation to the milestone plan, it may be because the conditions agreed upon in the project responsibility chart have not been adhered to. It may indeed be that the line management or other members of the base organisation are not supporting the project as agreed. If the chart is not followed, and it has implications for project progress, it is important that this be reported. The sponsor or management must be given an opportunity to decide on measures so that the responsibility chart will be followed (or possibly changed). An analysis from the project manager should always conclude with

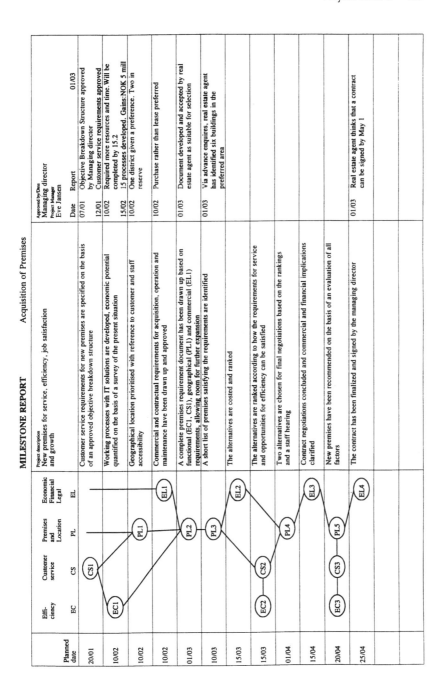

Figure 7.3 *Milestone report for the sub-project 'New premises for service, efficiency, job satisfaction and growth'*

a proposal for action, which the sponsor or steering committee can decide on.

Control is finding the actual causes for the deviation and proposing measures to do something about it.

Example of control at the milestone level

We are looking at the sub-project 'New premises for service, efficiency, job satisfaction and growth'. Figure 7.3 shows the milestone report for 1 March. The project may choose to report on the 1st of every month or when it falls on a Friday, the last working day before the 1st.

Important results and decisions are examined. Reports are also submitted for milestones that have been started but which will be completed later. It can also be explicitly stated whether the milestone has been reached and, if so, when. This has not been done in this report.

We should always report on what is known about the final milestone. In this case it could appear that there will be a small delay. This may mean that corrective measures should be evaluated.

In addition to the milestone report, it may be relevant for the project manager to submit a report against the project responsibility chart, with Yes/No checks for current control criteria.

Figure 7.4 shows what such a report may look like as of 1 March. Once more we see that the project has used more resources than planned.

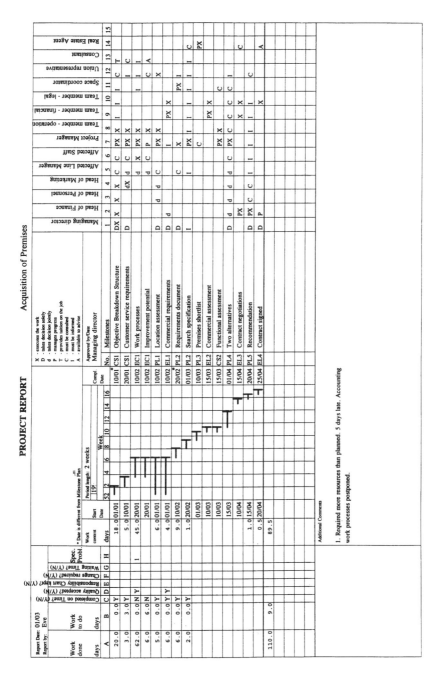

Figure 7.4 *Project (responsibility chart) report for the sub-project 'New premises for service, efficiency, job satisfaction and growth'*

8

Project Culture

By project culture we mean the base organisation's attitude to and understanding of the project work form. In this chapter we look at what characterises good project culture, and what can be done to improve it. We look at the role of the different actors in project work. We look at how the line management, steering committee, project management, project members and elected employee representatives should work together for more successful projects.

A GOOD PROJECT CULTURE

The project work form is becoming more and more important. This applies to both the public and private sectors.

Both government authorities and the business community are constantly facing new demands for change, development and improvement. Nowadays problems are complex and are rarely of such a nature that they can be resolved at one specific place in the base organisation. Many sections of the organisation must be involved. Change and development are complicated and unfamiliar concepts to many line managers. All-round expertise is required. At the same time problems must be resolved within a relatively short time span if the organisation is not to be weakened competitively or criticised by the public.

The most effective way to meet these challenges is to use the project work form. The ability to use this work form will be significant for the ability of a business to readjust, develop and improve itself. The quality of public operations and the survival of companies will depend on how well they will manage their projects.

A good project culture will be necessary. Project results should be delivered at the agreed time, with the agreed quality and within the agreed use of resources. Ideally, all projects should 'go like clockwork'. It should be possible to take a holiday with a clear conscience – with no project problems looming on the horizon.

This imposes demands on the whole organisation. This is not only a matter for the project manager and project members. Successful projects are dependent on support from all sectors of the organisation. Hence, the importance of project culture. A good project culture implies that:

❑ Everyone in the organisation understands the work form and what it requires by way of interaction between base organisation and project.
❑ Every project has good and binding plans, at both milestone and activity levels.
❑ Plans are controlled, so that everyone knows that variances are taken seriously.
❑ The project receives resources agreed upon from the base organisation.
❑ Decisions regarding professional matters are of the quality and within the deadlines agreed upon and to which the base organisation has committed itself.

Good project culture must permeate the whole system. Projects have a wide range, and everyone in an organisation is important for the project. Even if there is only one line manager or a few members of the base organisation who do not pull in the same direction or do not accept the project approach, it can have a damaging effect on the project.

A good project culture does not come about by itself. It is necessary to have a special development programme over a long period of time in order to achieve good results. Such programmes often begin by examining the project culture at the outset. We then see what it is particularly important to develop further in order to improve attitudes and skills.

In this book we are especially preoccupied with PSO projects and projects where project work is integrated into the base organisation. Project culture is particularly important for these types of projects, but it is also significant for other projects which at first glance do not appear to have the distinguishing features of a PSO project.

Large projects, for example, oil exploration in the North Sea and the Olympic Games at Lillehammer, are organised as separate organisations without a need to draw on resources from another base organisation. The base organisation versus project conflict is not encountered in this type of project. But even within these large projects there are individual projects which have the same characteristics and requirements as those with which we are particularly concerned.

Certain organisations, construction companies for example, implement tasks for others and use the project work form. They supply an end product to the sponsor of the project. It can be a purely technical product – a stretch of road or a bridge, for example. In this case there is probably not a very great need for cooperation between the sponsor organisation and the contractor's project organisation. The contractor will execute the project task on the basis of technical specifications and will supply the completed product. But if the contractor is to supply a solution to a problem which requires development within the sponsor's organisation, there must be mutual cooperation in order for benefits to be achieved.

We have a corresponding situation in the use of sub-contractors. The sub-contractor's task may be to supply a specified product, but the task may be broadened so that he has to perform development work which demands close cooperation between the two organisations. The sub-contractor's organisation then has a great need for cooperation with the sponsor's personnel.

A research and development project may require cooperation for long periods among a small group of researchers and developers. The group works closely together with little contact with the base organisation. But at a certain stage, we may hope, the project will present a product which must be developed for production and marketing, its profitability calculated, etc. The project then moves into a new phase, where contact with the base organisation will be intense.

These examples illustrate that projects very often have a need for contact with people working in a base organisation. Whether projects will be successful or not depends on a common understanding of the significance of the project and a common perception of how it should proceed. Therefore, project culture will be important, both in PSO projects and in projects which in the initial stages do not proceed like typical PSO projects.

A good project culture requires a joint effort from line management, steering committee, project management, elected employee representatives and anyone who performs a job, large or small, in the project. This interaction is absolutely fundamental. We will look first at the line management.

LINE MANAGEMENT

Line management will be involved in project work either because they have personnel responsibility for people who do jobs for the project, or because they will participate in or contribute to the professional decision-making processes in the project.

We will start with an instance where top management has prioritised and approved a project. It should be a part of their normal duty to the organisation that the line managers support the project, even if they themselves have not participated in the decision-making processes. Top management and line management must together disseminate information to the staff in the base organisation on the priorities behind the decisions to back these projects. They must create an understanding of why it is important to implement them.

The line manager's task is to carry through agreed commitments regarding the project. They mainly consist of making professional decisions at the right time and arranging for the agreed personnel resources to be made available for the project. The line managers must be loyal to whatever has been agreed upon and documented on the project and principle responsibility charts. They must support the project in word and deed.

When the project manager and the line management have worked out a responsibility chart and agreed that a specific decision-making process should take place during the last half of April, this really means that the decision should be made by 1 May. It should have been thoroughly discussed and each individual professional member affected should have had an opportunity to make his views known and should have accepted the decision taken. The line management must understand that delays create huge problems. The agreement also means that the decision is binding, except for certain unforeseen circumstances.

In PSO projects, most project members are subordinate to a line manager. This means that the project manager does not have the full authority to determine when they should work for the project. If access to personnel resources is not to be a major problem for the project manager, the line manager must see to it that people are available for the project as agreed. The line manager must ensure that others take over the project members' tasks in the base organisation. Release must be more than just a casual agreement; there must be a cover plan.

Participation in the project and project results are also important for the base organisation. Therefore the line manager must motivate his staff for the project. It ought to be routine that the contribution of the people from the base organisation to projects be assessed in their performance evaluations.

It is easy for line management to assert that they do not have resources to spare for project work. This is especially the case in organisations with a poorly developed project culture and with little understanding of the importance of change and development.

The problem is aggravated if there are only a few staff members who are regarded as possible project members. They will keep turning up like 'a bad penny' in connection with projects. An organisation that wants a good project culture and understands the importance of using the project approach should broaden its project expertise. By this means it will be able to draw on more members when it recruits people for project work.

If a company apparently does not have the resources for prioritised projects, the following questions may help promote discussion:

- There will have been large one-off tasks undertaken previously, even if they were not called projects. How were resources found for these?
- If there are such non-recurring tasks in progress at present, are they as important as priority projects the organisation now wants to undertake?
- Of all the non-recurring work, actual and potential, what are the priority tasks for the organisation?
- How are resources being used in the organisation? Are they being wasted, for example, in a non-productive meeting culture?

The organisation should realise the significance of development work and systematically make decisions to free resources for this kind of work.

A positive feature is that as a rule there is always room for some development work. Staff are often willing, eager in many cases, to participate in development projects. They see a project as a change and a challenge in comparison with their daily routine work, and they will make great efforts to be included in projects. Even if someone is fully occupied with daily work, it is still possible to become involved in project tasks, but this is not the most satisfactory solution. A good project culture means that resources for project work have high priority and are not based on goodwill.

STEERING COMMITTEE

Role and responsibility

A steering committee is the project manager's superior. It may also be called the management group. The steering committee plays a central role in a project. Its main responsibilities are to initiate and propose the project and approve the principle responsibility chart, the milestone plan and the project responsibility chart. It should determine the use of resources and ensure that the project responsibility chart and the principle responsibility chart are observed.

You could ask whether there is a need for a steering committee. If those in positions of responsibility are clearly delineated on the responsibility chart, and the role of the base organisation is clearly described, is a steering committee still necessary? In many cases it is. But in some cases we can manage without.

A significant issue for the project approach is that the project is dependent on resources from the base organisation. Even if it is absolutely clear which resources should be provided by it, in practice this is not always so easy to achieve. It can then be beneficial to have a steering committee, which should be a group of line managers, to ensure that the relationship between the base organisation and the project functions as it should. These line manager colleagues can see to it that everyone sticks to the agreements made, and can among themselves find solutions for problems which arise from time to time with access to resources. It may be easier for a group of line managers to tackle these problems than for a project manager to take them up with each line manager in turn.

What we have just said also shows who should be included in the steering committee, the line managers who are involved in the project. It is not normal practice, for instance, that elected employee representatives have a place in the steering committee.

If the project only involves the staff of one line manager, then it is natural that this line manager be the 'steering committee'. The responsibility chart shows that this manager is assigned all the operational tasks belonging to a steering committee.

Usually a project involves areas of responsibility and personnel belonging to several line managers. If the managers involved meet frequently as a manager group, it is best that this group, in addition to its other duties, also functions as a steering committee for the project. Part of the time of the management group's meeting should then be used as a steering committee meeting.

We see no reason to establish a new forum unless absolutely necessary. It simplifies administration, and it is clear that people who are used to working together in other matters function better as a group.

Some organisations have decided that their management board should function as a steering committee for all projects involving more than one sector. The board then makes time for steering committee tasks each time they assemble.

Some companies have so much experience using the project approach that it is regarded as hardly necessary to establish a steering committee function. Relevant tasks will then be divided among those involved according to their areas of responsibility and described on the responsibility charts.

We present two situations where a steering committee is essential. They are when:

❑ the project approach is unknown in the base organisation;
❑ the project crosses organisational limits or involves several companies.

If the organisation does not have any experience with project work it is particularly important to give prestige and support to the project and the project manager. This can be achieved to a greater extent by establishing a steering committee than distributing its tasks to a series of individuals. Since the steering committee consists of some or all line managers, it will be perceived as a forum with authority, and its pronouncements will be listened to.

If the line management is not used to working with projects, it is difficult in many cases to ensure that it will accept its responsibility for the project. When matters are discussed in a steering committee with several line managers, it is easier to get individual line managers to realise their responsibilities. Line managers are more aware of their responsibilities when they see that others also take on similar responsibilities. The same matters can, of course, be expressed on the responsibility charts, but the dialogue between the participants in a steering committee ensures that the commitments are more deeply felt.

In a company lacking project experience, training and motivation are important. It is particularly important that knowledge and expertise come in at the top level. In such a situation a steering committee can be used deliberately to provide training in project work. When central people in the base organisation belong to a steering committee, it can be used to give project members skills and shared attitudes.

If the project is a joint venture for several organisations, a steering committee is essential. One example could be that several firms within the same line of business join forces to purchase hardware and software to solve a common data-processing task. In such a case, one executive from a single organisation does not preside over the decision, but rather executives from all the companies collaborate on the project. Some decisions must be made jointly, and that requires a steering committee.

Let us look a little more closely at the steering committee's tasks. It will have tasks relating to the base organisation. First and foremost it should ensure that it lives up to its commitments. It should ensure that resources are released and the decisions made as agreed. The steering committee must:

❑ Ensure that the right people are chosen for the project tasks.
❑ Ensure that the project is prioritised on the basis of the organisation's needs, if circumstances arise in the base organisation that create resource problems and individual line managers want to curtail the project.
❑ Contribute to finding solutions if access to resources falters.
❑ Monitor that the decision-making processes in the base organisation function as agreed. It must be on guard against decisions made too slowly or too quickly and it must counteract tendencies among line managers to serve only their own interests.

The steering committee should carry out quality control for plans, progress, and results produced by the project manager and team. The steering committee must:

❑ Contribute to motivation and team spirit in the project.
❑ Acknowledge when milestones and project goals are reached. Rewards are often in short supply.
❑ Ensure that project management functions at a high level of quality.

From what has been said so far, it is clear that appointment to a steering committee is not an honorary title but an important job. The steering committee has management responsibility, a high level of responsibility for the project's success.

The steering committee should not make professional or technical decisions, but ensure that there are high quality plans and decision-making processes. It should assist the project manager by seeing to it that the decision-makers and resource-providers fulfil their obligations at the times agreed. This imposes considerable demands and expectations on the steering committee. The leader of the group has a special responsibility to make certain that it lives up to its responsibilities.

Good work on the part of the steering committee can be measured by a better project culture in the organisation.

Dangers

There is a fundamental difference between a *steering* committee and a *decision-making* group. In general we are against decision-making groups in project work. They imply that the people who have professional responsibility in the base organisation are deprived of that responsibility, that it is transferred instead to a group which is usually less competent than those who deal with such matters on a daily basis. The establishment of a decision-making group conflicts with one of the central principles for project work, namely that as far as possible professional decisions follow the normal decision-making process. A decision-making group has negative consequences both for the quality of decisions and for motivation in the base organisation to accept those decisions.

There is an acknowledged danger that a steering committee easily can develop into a decision-making group. This is the greatest problem with steering committees.

In many cases the people who are to make professional decisions belong to the steering committee. But it is important to state explicitly that when a line manager who also belongs to the steering committee makes decisions he is doing so as a line-manager – and not in the capacity of a member of the steering committee. And if there is a need for decisions to be made jointly by several line managers, where they all perhaps belong to the steering committee, then this decision should not be made within the framework of the steering committee's tasks. It is a group of line managers which is exercising its authority.

Even if we strongly emphasise that the steering committee should not make professional decisions which belong in the base organisation, it happens often nevertheless. It has serious consequences for the base organisation's attitude to the project, we get what we call 'denial of responsibility in the base organisation'. This means that it does not feel any commitment to the decisions made. Difficult decisions must often be made in a project. If a line manager feels that he can avoid making some decisions because the steering committee is encroaching on his territory, it is tempting for him to let this happen and just wait and see whether the decision was right or not.

It is easy for a line manager to push decisions which should be his responsibility over to the steering committee, if the steering committee does not adhere to the principle of keeping out of the base organisation's area of responsibility. You will then hear the chorus from the base organisation saying, 'But we've got a steering committee which makes all the decisions'.

If the steering committee is also a decision-making group, there will be a slow decision-making process. The problem is partly of a purely practical nature. It is a well-known phenomenon that it is difficult to get a lot of busy people together for a meeting, at least at short notice. At the same time it is a fact that once we have these meetings, the majority of decisions will be made there. There is thus a tendency for business to accumulate pending the next meeting. The result is that a considerable period of time passes before decisions are made.

Nevertheless, there are situations where it is proper for the steering committee also to function as a decision-making group. The most important case is when the project is a joint project for several independent organisations. Certain professional decisions have a great impact on the project costs, and since they will be distributed among several businesses, it is a matter for the steering committee to make a decision on professional questions that have a significant influence on costs.

In less critical matters one may establish decision-making groups with representatives from all the participating organisations, so that those who have daily responsibility for a particular area in their own group agree jointly on what is the best solution.

Operation of the steering committee

When a steering committee is established, it must not be assumed that it will know how to organise its work. Neither is it obvious that the participants have the necessary skills to perform the steering committee function. Often several participants in the steering committee have not done such work before. Project management differs from management of the base organisation. Experiences from normal line management cannot automatically be transferred to work in a steering committee.

Lack of perspective in steering committee work often leads to chance and unstructured discussions, continual conflicts of interest and advocacy of individual obsessions.

The steering committee often has a representative composition; it consists of those line managers who have interests in the project. They are people who represent the various parties involved in the project. They sometimes see taking care of the interests of their unit of the base organisation as being their main task. It can create a positive environment to hold a discussion to clarify different interests and matters of conflict as an introduction to the project. The fact that there are differing views on how strongly a project should be prioritised or on the direction it should take must not be regarded as being negative.

The milestone plan, with discussions on goals, and the project responsibility chart are tools which can be used to clarify special interests and to define precisely the participation of the different parties in the project. A high level of involvement in these discussions is to the good. But there is a problem if the steering committee is continually used for airing conflicts or promoting factional interests. This means that the same arguments are constantly cropping up. Individual parties do not accept the results produced during planning. The result will be that the steering committee will not make any progress. Instead of monitoring the progress of the project, it will become bogged down in a discussion of the high level questions that should have been clarified once and for all. The members of the steering committee will pursue their own interests instead of considering the project.

It is important to determine whether the steering committee has the necessary background to be able to function well. If the right conditions are not met, special training measures must be introduced.

As mentioned previously, project management and line management are two different things, and future steering committee participants – including those with extensive administrative experience – should not take it as a form of criticism or disparagement if they are given an introduction into the special tasks appropriate to a steering committee. For reasons of prestige, one can meet resistance to this. It is therefore wise to integrate the training into some form of start-up meeting for the project. In this way steering committee training is camouflaged because it occurs simultaneously with a number of other project activities.

The efficiency of the steering committee also depends on the project manager. The way the project manager uses the steering committee determines the results from its work. It is therefore important that the project manager has a clear picture of what constitutes matters for the steering committee. The project manager must himself be very certain of what the steering committee should work on, and – equally important – what it should not trouble itself with.

The project manager influences the steering committee's work by laying the foundation upon which the group's discussions are based. He must make sure that the steering committee receives documents in good time before a meeting and that each item on the agenda is thoroughly prepared. The project manager must actively contribute toward developing an efficient working style in the steering committee. It is expedient to have:

□ set days for meetings planned at least six months ahead;
□ certain permanent items on the agenda;
□ minutes with a predetermined structure.

It may seem to be a small practical detail that the steering committee should establish its meeting days for six months at a time, but this is no trivial matter. Participants in a steering committee are often people who are heavily burdened with meetings. It is important to set the steering committee meeting while the participants still have openings in their schedules. Furthermore it should be emphasised that missing a steering committee meeting has implications for project progress and makes the steering committee jointly responsible for any project delay. If the project is taken seriously, 'death and funerals' are just about the only valid grounds for absence from meetings.

Permanent items at all meetings contribute to establishing firmly the main tasks of the steering committee. This will help everyone understand that these are the central questions. In addition to permanent items, the agenda may, of course, also contain problems brought forward by project work since the last steering committee meeting, about which the group should be informed or required to make a decision.

At every steering committee meeting the project manager must keep the milestone plan and the responsibility charts alive by referring to them and relating them to all discussions.

It is important that the minutes be sent out relatively quickly after each meeting and that they state clearly the actions decided upon and who has been assigned the responsibility for executing them. This is vital for steering committee meetings. Late minutes can easily create the impression that 'there is no sense of urgency'. If the steering committee itself is not disciplined, it cannot expect others to be.

The minutes must state the steering committee's decisions (approved plans, changes to plans, actions, etc). The minutes are documents that project members will use in their work. It is of lesser importance to report the debate leading up to the decisions. This often contributes to very long reports and will also focus on disagreements within the steering committee, something which it is not necessary for the project team to know. In certain cases, however, it is necessary to report the background on which the decisions were taken, so those reading the reports understand and accept the decisions. We recommend that a set form is developed for the minutes, which makes them easy to read and easy for the project members to recognise.

Tasks

In the previous sections, we have spoken about a steering committee's tasks. We will conclude by relating the tasks to the tools that we suggest in this book. The steering committee should:

- ❑ Approve the project responsibility chart.
- ❑ Approve the principle responsibility chart (there may be one which applies generally to all projects in the organisation, in which case the steering committee does not need to discuss it).
- ❑ Approve the milestone plan.
- ❑ Be responsible for ensuring that the project follow the principle responsibility chart, project responsibility chart and the milestone plan.

The steering committee should be responsible for the global organisation of the project. The organisation is expressed by the project responsibility chart. It is therefore natural that the steering committee approve it. It must also take action if there is any variance from what has been agreed upon. It is the steering committee's responsibility to ensure that the project responsibility chart is followed.

It is not the steering committee's task to set up the project responsibility chart. The project manager does this in cooperation with the people and parties whom it is natural to draw in to the current project, but final approval rests with the steering committee.

The principle responsibility chart draws up guidelines for how project work will be conducted in the organisation. These guidelines may be applied to all the projects in the organisation, and should be authorised by the organisation's top management.

On the principle responsibility chart it may be specified that certain project decisions should be taken by the steering committee. This applies especially to questions concerning the project's goals, limitations and finances.

It is the steering committee's task to approve the milestone plan and be sure that it is followed. The milestone plan is the most important planning document in the project and it is natural that the steering committee, as the project's top authority, is responsible for it. In following up the milestone plan, the steering committee carries out its central progress control function. If the plan cannot be followed, the steering committee must decide whether changes should be made in the milestone plan, or whether corrective measures should be introduced. It is the project manager who is responsible for preparing the basis for the steering committee's decisions. This applies both to the milestone plan and the milestone reports upon which control is based.

PROJECT MANAGER

The project manager manages the project on a day to day basis. He must plan the work, organise it and ensure that corrective measures are taken, so that the project is finished within time and budget. The project manager must also re-evaluate the plan if access to resources is not as expected.

The project manager must organise work internally within the project and in relation to the base organisation. He must arrange for effective interfaces between the project and the base organisation.

The project manager must anticipate events. He cannot expect that project members will just pop up when the project needs them. He must plan, negotiate with line managers, motivate, inspire, conclude agreements on cooperation in the project and see to it that the resources appear at the right time.

Project management is different from line management, and it demands other skills. This book is an introduction to methods and tools which are used in project work and which are usually unfamiliar to line managers.

It is a characteristic trait of project work that the project manager manages people who do not work together on a daily basis, and therefore do not know each other in the same way as colleagues in the base organisation. The project manager must create a sense of common cause among people who originally are strangers.

Project management should be regarded as a distinct profession requiring specialised knowledge and skills. Most people accept the fact that you cannot become a line manager until you have gone through a basic 'apprenticeship' where you acquire the relevant knowledge, experience and interpersonal insight. But it is depressing to see – even in organisations which set high standards for line management – how the same standards are not applied to project managers, even for very important projects.

Too little effort goes into developing good project managers. Since project management is probably more difficult in general than line management (because of unknown tasks and unfamiliar people), higher requirements for training and experience should actually be set for a project manager than for a line manager.

The project manager should be educated in the field of project management. It is now possible to acquire basic professional skills through courses and training programmes. Experience as a 'rank and file' project member is also necessary.

An organisation should spend time and money training its project managers. You cannot be a line manager without a solid background – some believe that anybody can be a project manager.

Qualities

One sometimes see specifications for the personal qualities required of a project manager. He should, for example, have distinct leadership qualities (charisma), be respected by his team, have the ability to communicate with superiors and subordinates and be able to represent the project externally in a favourable manner. Such lists often give a picture of a person who is superhuman, and are usually of little practical use. There

is no sense in dreaming away and demanding supernatural qualities of a project manager. When an organisation must choose a
project manager for a project, it is necessary to choose from
among those who are available.

The project manager's personal character is important, but for
most practical purposes there is little value in comparing a
person with a list of super qualities. Instead it is important to
have an idea of the essential requirements for a project
manager's success. And since it is often extremely difficult to
know whether a person will succeed as a project manager, it is
also useful to know what type of person should be avoided
absolutely.

A project manager must be capable of formulating a realistic
description of the present situation in the project. At the same
time he must be able to manage if there is a variance between
what the present situation is and what it should be. He should also
have the ability to see what types of measures will be effective.

The project manager must observe progress in the project
very closely. He must be able to assess the situation realistically.
A dreamer (who only sees through rose-coloured glasses) or an
optimist (who believes that everything will sort itself out as it
goes along) is of no use.

Realism in the evaluation of the present situation must apply
to both factual matters and people. The reporting proformas
which we described earlier are, of course, very useful tools for
developing an accurate description of the present situation. They
are first and foremost factual, that is they report developments in
relation to the project's plans and goals. They are to a lesser
degree oriented to the welfare of the team. The project manager,
on the other hand, must be concerned with both factual matters
and people. He must be able to sense the mood of the project
and form a realistic picture of the team members' situation. He
must support them and assist them in the realisation of the
goals. Assisting means pushing reserved people forward and
controlling dominant ones.

In general, a project manager must be flexible by nature, so
that he will be able to change course along the way. He must be
action-oriented, that is he must be willing to try new measures if

there is a deviation between the plan and reality. Through a constant evaluation of what works and what does not work, including his own contributions, helpful or not, a project manager can continually improve his competency.

We hope that we have not just described a new superhuman. We do not believe so. We have indicated how important it is that the project manager:

❑ gives a realistic assessment of the project situation, concerning both factual matters and people;
❑ proposes and implements actions to correct situations, concerning both factual matters and people;
❑ learns what types of measures are effective, concerning both factual matters and people.

An important aspect of the choice of project manager is to avoid a person who is not really suited for the job. We will describe three types who are dangerous for any project. They are the technocrat, the bureaucrat and the salesman. The descriptions below will perhaps seem to be caricatures, but they contain important truths.

First a little about the technocrat. The most able programmer seldom makes a good project manager for an IT project. He is so preoccupied with programming skills that he has neither the time, desire nor ability to practice project management. Project management does *not* mean doing the job yourself, but seeing to it that others do. Super-technocrats are dangerous as project managers because they believe – with some reason – that they can do everything best themselves. They do not actually want others to interfere in the work. They also often lack the personal qualities which enable them to get people to pull together as a group. The technocrat's strength lies at the technical level – not at the human level. Able technocrats are very important in projects, but not as project managers.

The bureaucrat is the person who regards project administration as being the essence of the project. He loves forms and reports. He is obviously a torment to those around him, especially those who do not follow procedures to the letter. Worse, however, is that he does not make any worthwhile use of all this paperwork. It does not form the basis for any action, it just accumulates in filing cabinets. When project members feel that reports are more important than the product they are producing, motivation falls drastically.

The salesman is the project manager who is all talk. Externally the project is presented as a real success – internally little is happening. It is obviously important to maintain the project's public profile and to create enthusiasm for and interest in it. Yet all the talk is wasted if the project manager does not manage to follow it up with concrete plans and action. Unfortunately, there are far too many examples of projects that remain 'castles in the air'.

Tasks

The project manager's main tasks are summarised in Figure 8.1.

Planning tasks

Project level: Manage development of the milestone plan
Activity level: Manage development of the detail plans (the activity responsibility charts)

Organisational tasks

Project level: Manage development of the project responsibility chart
Activity level: Manage daily operations

Control tasks

Project level: Prepare the milestone reports
Monitor that the principle responsibility chart and the project responsibility chart are being followed
Activity level: Follow up on the activity reports

Figure 8.1 *The project manager's main tasks*

The tasks are listed under the headings of planning, organisation and control. There is a distinction between tasks at project level and activity level. Tasks at project level involve the project manager's work with the steering committee or whomever is fulfilling a corresponding function; tasks at activity level include his work with the project team.

The central project planning task is to draw up the milestone plan. This is the project manager's responsibility. Final approval lies with the steering committee.

At the activity level the project manager's main task is to manage the development of the activity plans, those plans which cover the activities between two milestones. In addition, he must involve himself in discussions on how the individual activities should be done, along with those who will actually carry them out.

Global organisation of the project is a significant task for the project manager. He has to develop a proposal for a project responsibility chart and present it to the steering committee for approval. The project manager leads the daily operations in the project. It is his task to ensure that work goes on day to day. He is responsible for prioritising and assigning tasks when this is not made clear by the plans. He must motivate and support his team.

A project manager should have professional qualifications in the field covered by the project, although there may be exceptions in very large projects. We feel that the project manager should be an 'active coach'; he should be able to direct and perform special work related to his professional area. This does not mean that he should be able to do more than everyone else, but he should be sufficiently qualified to be able to lead professional discussions in the project. We believe that a project manager who is unfamiliar with the professional issues in the project will lack the respect of his team.

The project manager must be able to guarantee the quality of the results produced by the project. In order to be able to do this he should preferably have a professional background which will enable him to judge the quality of the results. (Note that there is a great difference between performing a job and judging its quality; there is a difference between ski-jumping and awarding marks for the style of the jump.) In certain areas it may be appropriate that others carry out quality control. Nevertheless, it is essential that the project manager has a background that enables him to see the difference between good and poor quality.

The project manager must see that the project responsibility chart is followed in the project work. He must report the variances that he cannot correct himself to the steering committee.

The project manager must present milestone reports to the steering committee. There may be several reasons for variances between a milestone plan and the actual project situation. The project manager has the authority to put some matters right himself. Others must be submitted to the steering committee or the appropriate decision authority.

The project manager has a duty to tell the steering committee that a project should be terminated if he considers that it cannot achieve its goals. If they act on this recommendation, they must also actively support the project manager. He must not be made a scapegoat when he has done his duty and taken the initiative to stop in time.

The project manager also has a duty to inform the steering committee of the consequences for progress of an ill-judged choice of project members by the base organisation.

Controlling the activities is the project manager's responsibility. Project members provide the project manager with the basis he needs for his activity reports. He must take the initiative himself to iniate action if reports indicate deviation from the plan.

We have concentrated on the hard aspects of the project manager's tasks. In addition we strongly emphasise the project manager's responsibility for the 'climate' in the project. This means being concerned both with the situation of individual team members and the interaction between them.

The project manager is responsible for developing the project team. This is, perhaps, the most important job of all. He must stimulate, motivate, and secure cooperation from day to day so that everyone helps each other in their efforts to achieve common goals. He must get everyone involved in the project –

steering committee, the top executives, the line managers, project members, elected trade union representatives – to work together *for* the project. This task is not as clearly structured as the tasks we examined earlier in this section – but it is at least as important.

Where there is a spirit of community in a project, where everyone is prepared to help each other and to find solutions for delays instead of allocating blame, an important cooperative goal has been reached. This demands great things of project management. It demands a motivating and supportive management style, not an authoritarian one.

Permanent project manager?

This is an issue that only troubles larger businesses constantly engaged with some sort of development work. They face the question of whether they should have permanent project managers. The alternative is to let the project manager return to his usual job in the base organisation, at least, for a time.

Permanent project managers have both advantages and drawbacks. The advantages are very clear. The project managers expand their knowledge of and gain broad experience in project management. As permanent project managers they have greater opportunities to use what they have learned in a succession of projects. With a permanent group of project managers it is also possible to put into effect measures aimed at professionalising project management. By having the same project managers for several projects, all the projects in the business will benefit from a more uniform approach. It will become easier to exchange experience between projects and to use the experience from one project to achieve still better results in the next.

A project manager who gains experience from several types of project and from different areas within an organisation will also gradually acquire a deeper understanding of the base organisation's culture. He will see how the organisation functions and how management is exercised at different levels. The project manager thus has a good background for formulating proposals for solving problems within the organisation; he understands what *can* be done, and what will work.

One drawback of permanent project managers is that they become an institution in the organisation. In this position they acquire power or influence and in many situations it becomes natural to ask for their opinions. If they become too highly institutionalised, antagonism can easily develop between them and the rest of the base organisation. This is a poor basis for cooperation when a new project gets under way.

Previously we have stressed the importance of a project manager having professional expertise within the field of the project. When permanent project managers manage all projects within the business, you may have project managers who have little or no professional connection with the area of the project. This is a defect which must be balanced against the advantages of having a trained project manager.

A decision must be made on where to place permanent project managers in the base organisation. There are two alternatives:

❑ Under different line managers, at the same time functioning as a group.
❑ In a joint staff unit, which can, for example, come under the managing director.

The latter solution has the advantage that it is easier to professionalise project management.

ELECTED REPRESENTATIVES

In some countries, laws give elected employee representatives the right to joint consultation in development projects that alter the content and organisation of the work place.

Further, there can be a range of different forums and official bodies that ought to have a role in certain projects. We mention:

❑ the trade union (sometimes several).
❑ a work environment committee.
❑ a health and safety committee.

The groups vary from business to business. Their roles also differ greatly; some are established by formal agreement; others are more dependent on practices in the individual organisation.

Practice varies widely from country to country also. In some places, employee representatives assume responsibilities which would be culturally unacceptable elsewhere.

Therefore it must be up to each organisation and each project to determine roles and responsibilities. Unless these are made clear the employees' representatives may not acquire a role anywhere and may be omitted from the project.

If the elected representatives are to fulfil their responsibilities as such, they must choose carefully their areas of activity. In unstructured projects there is a tendency for the elected representatives to try to be a part of everything. In part they fear that something will happen behind their backs, and in part they have not thought through what they ought to concentrate on.

There are four matters which ought to be of particular interest for elected representatives:

❑ priorities for proposed projects and decisions on which projects should be started.
❑ the principle responsibility chart.
❑ the milestone plan, especially in projects which have an impact on future employment.
❑ the project responsibility chart.

The first two apply to project work in general, while the last two are linked to individual projects.

An organisation's projects are of decisive significance for its future. It is natural that the employees' representatives have views on which projects the organisation ought to prioritise.

The principle responsibility chart shows the main division of tasks in projects. The various employee interest groups must be assigned the correct roles.

The milestone plan with its result paths shows what the project should achieve. The employees' representatives must have an opportunity to put their views forward on project objective. They ought to pay particular attention to whether or not the plan takes into consideration anything affecting future employment.

The detailed responsibilities of elected representatives as set out in the project responsibility chart will vary greatly according to national and organisational practice as well as the specifics of the project. They may be consulted on a wide range of issues concerning employment and the working environment and these will be reflected in 'C's in the chart. This does not confer powers of decision or veto, of course, and if the representatives do not agree with what is decided, they may take it up with top management outside the context of the project organisation.

Some elected representatives misunderstand their function and believe that they should be included as much as possible – even at meetings where the detailed technical matters are discussed. This impairs their ability to do the real job they have in the project.

The danger of an elected representative being preoccupied with detail is greater when the person concerned has experience and expertise in the particular area within which the project is working. Elected representatives are drawn from the base organisation and are often very capable within their fields. Many are therefore tempted to express opinions on how detail activities ought to be executed. This is a clear misuse of the role of elected representative. It may be relevant to draw on their specific expertise, but that is in a completely different context. In that event, it should be stressed that the person concerned is acting as a professional consultant or as a future user. It is very important that an elected representative who is used in this way does not confuse this task with his role as elected representative.

9

Quality in Project Work

In the previous chapter we dealt with the organisational and human prerequisites necessary for successful projects. In this chapter we will look at what else we can do to secure project quality.

SIGNIFICANCE FOR THE ORGANISATION

Why is quality important in project work? A silly question perhaps, but it is always important to know what you wish to achieve before starting to take action.

We want quality in project work because it has benefits for the entire organisation; high quality in project work improves the base organisation. We can distinguish between two categories of projects which affect quality in organisations in different ways:

❑ Projects where the results change operations in the base organisation; this means that the quality of the project has direct consequences for the quality of the organisation.
❑ Projects where the results are delivered to an external sponsor and the quality of the results determines whether or not the base organisation has fulfilled its terms of delivery; this means that the quality has significance for the organisation's reputation and provides opportunities for future contracts.

The first type of project is a typical PSO project. It is intended to create change in the base organisation; it should improve it. The project raises the quality of the organisation. The better the quality of the project, the more the quality of the business is improved.

For such projects there are stringent requirements to be precise in describing what the project is to achieve and to be certain that it can be achieved. Project management must thus facilitate a thorough discussion of the project objective. It must also manage the interaction between the base organisation and the project, because the results will be created in the base organisation.

With projects that are intended to improve operational quality in the base organisation, you must in every case state in concrete terms what you wish to achieve, and how the operation will be changed. In the next chapter we introduce the objective breakdown structure – a systematic method to obtain an overview of the objectives the project will tackle. It can be an important tool in project quality assurance.

Our relocation example illustrated the importance of a good description of what is to be achieved. The company will not achieve an improvement in quality by moving if everything remains as before. Before relocation there must be a thorough exploration of the objectives of the move. Plans must focus on what results are desired and how they will be achieved. The project plans must stress cooperation, training and development of new attitudes. The project will be successful if it results in fewer customer complaints and claims, increased sales and greater accuracy in deliveries.

In PSO projects the main point is not to create a physical product. It is therefore more difficult to follow progress in these projects than where something physical gradually develops, such as bridges, roads or factories. In PSO projects, documents that indicate the project's achievements in all areas under development must be presented at agreed times. Project results must be constantly evaluated in order to ascertain whether we are on the right course. This is an important part of quality assurance.

Certain businesses exist by managing projects for others. Examples are consultancy firms, research and development organisations, construction companies and IT companies which supply 'tailor-made' products. For these, quality in project management is absolutely essential for their ability to survive. If they do not deliver the results as agreed, their reputation in the market will be seriously damaged.

Their projects differ from internal development projects because at the outset there is often a previously defined requirement specification. That means that their project management methods need not focus so much on identifying project needs. It is more important to be sure that the project always keeps to the requirement specifications, and that schedules and budget are adhered to.

It is increasingly the case, however, that businesses of this kind are also involved in establishing the project objectives and in implementing the desired results in the customer company. Then the emphasis in project management returns to accurate and complete definition of project objectives.

PROCEDURES

In order to achieve high quality in project work, it is necessary to introduce standardised procedures.

We will not go into the details of the procedures but we will show examples of areas where it is important to have set them and we will illustrate their purpose.

The content of the quality assurance procedures depends on whether they are drawn up for internal development projects or for customer supply projects. In the latter case, there are extended requirements in certain areas, such as entering into and complying with contracts. In practice, each business which uses the project approach must develop and document its own procedures.

We differentiate between two classes of procedures:

❑ procedures which are linked to specific phases in a project;
❑ fixed periodic procedures, usually monthly.

The following are examples of areas in which procedures are required.

To prioritise internal development projects

This procedure must be performed once a year and the results must be reviewed if substantial new factors appear. The purpose is to prioritise projects and not to allow chance to dictate which projects will be started. The procedure presupposes that the organisation has mapped its own resource situation, so that it knows what it can use for development objectives. By prioritising and maintaining an overview of the resource situation, management always has a current picture of what must be done if the project efforts must be reduced or new, more important, development needs crop up.

To formulate goals and results (draw up a project mandate)

This procedure must be performed early in the project. It is repeated when the situation dictates, for example when there are essential changes in circumstances. A complete, regularly updated project mandate ensures that the project works on the right things.

To divide the project into phases, sub-projects, etc

This procedure is performed early in the project. The purpose is to provide a foundation for better planning. The procedure ensures that plans are not made for larger sections than can be mastered. During division, the goals for each section (phase or sub-project) must be described and the resource requirement roughly estimated.

To start each project section by drawing up a milestone plan and a responsibility chart

This procedure is performed at the start of each project section. The purpose is that all core project members acquire a common understanding of tasks and project progress and can commit their own input. Moreover, people should agree on which milestones are especially critical to the project so that everyone understands the serious consequences if these milestones are not reached in time or are realised with poor quality.

To conclude each project section with an evaluation

This procedure is performed at the conclusion of each project section. The purpose is to evaluate the results achieved against the milestones, the resource input against the estimates, and the implementation of the responsibility chart. A summary of changes, additions, and obstacles should be developed. Capturing this kind of experience will be useful in the project and contribute to ensuring quality in the long run.

To conclude the whole project with an evaluation

This procedure is carried out at the end of the project. The purpose is to analyse systematically the final results of the project in relation to the project's stated goals and result requirements.

To hold monthly project meetings

This procedure is performed at least once a month. The purpose is that all current project members – and they alone – should meet to report, agree on making up delays, activity plan the next milestones, and hold discussions on professional matters and on quality requirements in particular. Each member should commit his own activities and his input. They must be sure to obtain renewed acceptance for their input into the project from their line managers.

To obtain acceptance in the steering committee for progress and action

This procedure is performed a short time after the project meeting. The purpose is to obtain acceptance for what has been agreed upon at the project meeting concerning project progress and proposals for actions that will affect future progress.

PLANNING DOCUMENTS

From the organisation's point of view it is essential that planning documents be accurate and usable. Poor plans lead to failing interest in the planning documents as instruments for management. Good plans are necessary if problems in reporting are to be avoided.

It is too late if defects in the plans are discovered after the project has started. The damage has been done and time has run out. We therefore recommend that plans should be subject to quality assurance before they are approved.

204   Goal Directed Project Management

Quality assurance can take place in several ways. One or more competent individuals can go through the plans together with the project manager. Or the plans can be circulated for comment so that the participants are given an opportunity to offer their opinions of them.

Under no circumstances must the project manager assume a defensive attitude. A difficult situation arises if there is a fundamental flaw in the plan and the project manager is not willing to recognise it. A common answer from the project manager in such cases is: 'This is the best that can be done' or 'You do not understand the situation – the sponsor of the project wants a simple plan, not your sophisticated affair.'

This type of reaction arises when we are working on improving quality. We should have a policy established in advance that outlines how we will deal with a situation where someone feels that the plans are inadequate. It may take time to draw up a better plan – but it is possible.

We have developed a checklist for use in quality assurance of plan documents. It is shown in Figure 9.1.

The milestone plan

*   Instead of the present milestone plan, should there be several milestone plans because many of the milestones have nothing to do with each other?
*   Does the plan ensure that the project creates something of worth for the base organisation?
*   Does the plan contribute to raising the quality of the project?
*   Do the result paths reflect what we want to achieve by the project work? (Avoid general result areas or result areas which express organisation units.)
*   Does the plan ensure that important decisions are made?
*   Is the completion date acceptable?
*   Is the plan correctly balanced, ie is the degree of detail the same throughout the whole plan?
*   Does the plan facilitate parallel progress? (Avoid, if possible, a 'relay', ie a sequence where all tasks follow one after the other)
*   Does the plan have a clear structure, correct sequence, logical dependencies and clear layout?

The individual milestone

* Is the description of the milestone such that it is intelligible outside the project group, ie for affected line managers and others in the base organisation?
* Is quality assurance built into the description?
* Is approval of quality specified in the description?
* Are there references to methods which can ensure quality?
* Can we ascertain whether the milestone has been reached?
* For plans and milestones where creativity is important: Is the description neutral as to the solution?
* Are quantitative goals built into the description where possible?

The responsibility charts

* Does the division of responsibility reflect the real situation, or is it based on wishful thinking?
* Are there more parties/bodies or responsibilities than can be dealt with? In other words, will progress suffer if the responsibility chart is followed?
* Is the division of roles such that quality will be assured?
* Are important external relationships recognised?
* Have planned absences and possible illness been taken into consideration?
* Have interruptions and other work tasks been taken into consideration when the tasks have been put into calendar time?
* Are any of the resources unrealistically hard pressed?
* Has the fact that decision-making processes take time been taken into consideration?

When the plan is unrealistic

* Can the tasks be redistributed?
* Can the scope be reduced?
* Can more resources be introduced into the project?
* Can the milestone plan be changed – ie is it possible to do the work in a completely different way?

Figure 9.1 *Checklist for quality assurance of documents in project work*

RISK ASSESSMENT

It is important to assess risks in a project. A project undertakes to create results of a certain quality within time and resource constraints. But will it succeed? What risks are involved in the project that may make it difficult to achieve its goals? It is here that risk assessment is useful.

Inadequate procedures for quality assurance and poor quality plans – matters which we have looked at in the previous sections – create a great risk for unpleasant surprises in the course of the project. But there are many other sources of risk in project work.

We will suggest some areas that must be considered when assessing risks. We do not pretend that the list is complete; conditions vary greatly from project to project. The intention is to identify some of the aspects of projects that are particularly exposed to risk, so that the project manager can assess whether he wants to take action. We suggest that:

- ❏ The plan itself may have aspects of risk.
- ❏ Technical areas of high risk must be identified.
- ❏ Decisions are often critical for progress.
- ❏ Resource requirement estimates are always an area of risk.
- ❏ Access to resources is often uncertain in a project.

Figure 9.2 is a checklist of factors which can be used to assess the risks in a project.

The plan itself may have aspects of risk

* When the completion date is an absolute deadline, the risk assessment must be as comprehensive as possible. In addition, the possibilities for reducing the level of ambition along the way should be evaluated, in case you fall behind schedule.
* Projects often have a tendency to have a slow start, while the progress plan is based on a fast pace from Day One. What does it mean if we lose time at the start? What can we do to maintain the pace from the start?
* Can we count on complete loyalty to the plan from the base organisation, or will we meet resistance? What is likely to be most controversial, and what can we do to counteract resistance?

* Will the project be regarded as important by the project members, or will they downgrade project work in favour of everyday base organisation work?
* Is the progress plan based on a realistic view of resource requirements, access to resources and calendar time? Have we drawn up a project plan which may break down unacceptably in total or in specific periods?

The technical areas of risk must be identified

* Have we managed to describe and scope the project in such a way that we are sure that it will not grow out of control?
* Is the technology one that is new to us? Can we do anything to control it in such a way that we do not expose the project to unacceptable risks?
* There may be milestones which are not clear and which express several intentions rather than one clearly described state. Does this apply to any milestones in our plan, and how critical are they?
* Are we particularly vulnerable in certain areas if we do not obtain all the required expertise? Can we do anything about it?
* What technical aspects of the plan are especially critical with regard to project progress and the quality of the project results? Can we do anything to reduce the risk?

Decisions are often critical for progress

* Which decisions are most *important* in the project? What happens if it becomes clear that a decision must be made again? What are the consequences of this for progress and costs?
* Which decisions are most *critical* in the project? What happens if we do not obtain these decisions in time? What happens if they must be made again?
* Have we allotted a realistic interval from completion of a report until decisions made upon it? Have all the 'd's and 'D's understood what it means to be allocated these symbols? Have all the decision makers checked that they are available during the decision-making period?

* Is the base organisation's culture such that you can count on obtaining lasting decisions or are decisions regularly ducked or postponed?
* Too many 'D's, 'd's and 'C's on the responsibility chart make management of the decision-making process an impossible task for the project manager and an area of risk for the project. Can the project live with the decision-making structure and still meet deadlines? The same may apply to an individual milestone so that it becomes an element of risk.
* Can we reckon on encountering 'trip-wires' because someone does not want the project results? Or because they run counter to this person's hopes and expectations?
* Are any decisions sensitive and confidential, and can they create difficulties for open communication in the project?

Estimates of resource requirement are vulnerable to risk

* Which estimates are most critical in relation to elapsed time? When assessing risks is it sufficient to concentrate on the milestones which require a high level of resource input?
* Does a systematic method of approach lie behind the estimates – or is it just a case of 'think of a number'? Are the estimates arrived at through a recommended procedure?
* Who has drawn up the estimate? Is it one person or several? Is it likely that someone has given artificially low estimates to obtain approval for the project?
* It may be necessary to obtain minimum and maximum estimates for the activities most exposed to risk. This gives an indication of the sensitivity of those activities.

Access to resources is often uncertain in a project

* Which parts of the plan are most critical with regard to access to resources?
* Are there certain parts of the base organisation which have a habit of never providing the agreed resources at the agreed time? What can we do about it?

Figure 9.2 *Factors when assessing project risks*

A PROJECTIVITY PROGRAMME

Projectivity is an organisation's ability to achieve new goals and results using a project approach. The word (which was first used by the Swede, Torbjörn Wenell) is designed to provide associations with the words effective, productivity and project. If the organisation is to improve its projectivity, it must work consciously toward this goal. In this section we will look more closely at the elements of a projectivity programme, in other words, we will look at a development plan to improve projectivity in the base organisation.

The following conditions must always exist for such a programme to be successful.

The programme must be supported by the organisation's top management

Support means something more than management deciding that the programme should be started. It should also have understood what the programme implies by way of involvement for themselves and others. They must really want such a programme because they realise the importance of mastering the project work form.

A project manager must be designated for the programme

There must be one person who has experience both as a project manager and with GDPM as a method. He must have easy access to top management and command great respect of the project managers in the organisation.

The programme must be planned and organised like other projects

It must be divided up into phases and have a duration of at least a year. All projects that are at an appropriate stage of development must be included, ie those which have reached a stage where a milestone plan and a responsibility chart can be drawn up. The worst thing is to select simple, small projects as tests. They will not receive the necessary attention. In any case, the real problems will not be revealed. If the number of projects

210 Goal Directed Project Management

must be limited, at least do not exclude the most important, the largest and the most difficult ones.

Before launching a projectivity programme, a certain amount of groundwork must be done. Top management must have approved a foundation which forms the basis for all project work in the organisation. It must specify at least:

- The organisation's purpose for using the project work form.
- Policies for project work, in other words the fundamental guidelines for directing each project.
- The chosen method for directing project work (we presuppose that GDPM be chosen).
- The various procedures to be followed in project work.
- Documentation requirements for project work.

The document which describes the foundations for project work should apply to the whole organisation – line management, line members, project management and project members – and also to external collaborating parties. It is the common basis for project work and also expresses how project quality will be assured within the base organisation. It states the level of ambition and provides the framework for the projectivity programme.

At an early stage in the work on improving projectivity, the organisation's project culture should be mapped. One must understand what hinders and what promotes projectivity in the existing project culture. Different projects in the organisation must be examined. There are often great dissimilarities between the different categories of project (product development, computer and organisation development projects, for example, and purely technical projects). There may also be great differences in maturity in relation to project work in different parts of the base organisation.

It may be relevant to:

- ask all workers to fill out a questionnaire;
- interview a representative selection from the various categories of people.

The results will reveal the base organisation's project culture. They provide a basis for proposing actions and provide a direction for further work in the projectivity programme.

An organisation cannot implement such a programme with too many project managers. It may be necessary to limit the number, both to achieve a manageable development programme and to secure high quality project managers. On the other hand neither can an organisation have too few trained project managers. They ought to have a professional connection with the area within which their projects are working – and that requires a number of project managers who actively use the project approach. Reorganisation of project management, good organisational support and selection of the best project managers are normally important elements in a successful programme.

Project managers receive special treatment in a projectivity programme and will be the recipients of a structured development programme. The purpose is to bring the project managers up to a fully professional level in planning, organisation, control, team development and base organisation cooperation.

As a link in the development programme the project managers should work on arranging the next year's prioritisation of the organisation's many projects. The project manager forum can also serve as a review group for new milestone plans and responsibility charts.

It may be appropiate to give formal certification to project managers when they have reached a desired level of proficiency. Certification should be carried out by an independent body. It should inspect the finished projects and their results. The project manager's input should be judged on the basis of the quality of:

❑ milestone plans and responsibility charts;
❑ activity planning;
❑ progress reporting to management;
❑ project control, at project level and activity level;
❑ team development in the project;
❑ relationships with line managers;
❑ handling of the decision-making process.

When top management has initiated a projectivity programme, it must also take an interest in it and follow up its results. The project manager for the programme must make it easy for management to involve itself in the work. There should be at least one meeting a month between the project manager and top management, where the progress of the programme and current projects included in it are dealt with.

The line managers in the organisation must also be enabled to play their part; they can raise the quality of project plans by expressing their views and ideas. They can contribute to securing quality in project work by taking decisions as agreed and ensuring that their people are released for project work to the agreed extent and at the time agreed. They should cooperate closely with the project managers, both as a means of helping in the various projects, but also as a means of helping to develop and strengthen the managers themselves as a part of the projectivity programme.

For those parts of the organisation where initial studies showed a poorly developed project culture, it may be relevant to initiate a small development programme within the framework of the projectivity programme. This may apply to departments or groups where there is a need to build up respect for deadlines and quality of work. They may also require assistance in such things as drawing up plans and taking action to release resources.

Project meetings in individual projects are important forums for team development. The programme's project manager should participate in these meetings as a process adviser and observer. The project participants must be encouraged to take up questions which concern team working and relationships, and to find a solution for such problems jointly. The group must be trained to be more disciplined and structured in their methods.

All people in the base organisation should be offered a course in project methods. For line managers and their subordinates this may require one or two days.

The projectivity programme must be evaluated along the way by assessing quarterly individual project results and status. It is particularly important to determine whether:

- ❏ Completion dates are being adhered to.
- ❏ Resources brought in agree with the original estimates.
- ❏ The level of ambition remains the same or whether the project has been expanded or reduced.

Besides this, an assessment should be made of whether the project culture has improved. At the conclusion of the formal projectivity programme it may be relevant to do a further review of project culture like the one carried out as an introduction to the programme.

10

Objective Breakdown Structure

We have emphasised a number of times the fundamental importance of objectives as the basis for a project, but we have said little about how these objectives can be developed. Now we introduce the objective breakdown structure as a way of doing this.

The objective breakdown structure will help us to determine what the project should do for the base organisation. It gives us a picture of the project's possible results.

Formulating the project's outcome is a part of project work. You cannot expect the sponsor to state this precisely. The project itself must contribute by clarifying goals and anticipated results. This is not easy, especially when the project is extensive and complex, and the starting point is nothing more specific than a 'good idea'. The formulation of the goals often perpetuates the good intentions. They may have significant omissions in that essential matters have not been considered and discussed.

Since we describe objectives that must be achieved, and not how we achieve them, we can develop objectives at the introductory stage of a project.

In the following we will deal with:

- ❏ The purpose of an objective breakdown structure.
- ❏ The development of the objective breakdown structure.

We will begin, however, by showing the objective breakdown structure for our relocation example, so that you can immediately form a picture of its use.

THE RELOCATION EXAMPLE

We have drawn up milestone plans and responsibility charts for our comprehensive example. When clarifying the extent and direction of the project, we had as a starting point an objective breakdown structure, but we have not shown it before now.

An objective breakdown structure for this type of project must describe the part of the business (the base organisation) which the project is intended to serve. The objective breakdown structure is shown in Figure 10.1.

To strengthen our market position and profitability through total management of customer service and supply in a service-oriented building						
To provide financially and legally for planned and future growth **1**	To have a secure building which makes it easy to be our customer **2**	To ensure customers experience quality in all aspects of customer mangement **3**	To ensure quality and accuracy in supply of goods and services **4**	To commit all staff through our public commitment to customers **5**	To reorganise the work and introduce new skills **6**	To introduce effective work processes and administrative support **7**
Ensure we work within agreed budgets for investments and operation **11**	Provide a welcoming building **21**	Institute policies and standards for customer service **31**	Ensure we keep our promises on all orders **41**	Provide effective product information **51**	Organise work around individual responsibility for customers **61**	Develop effective work processes and IT solutions **71**
Secure good access for customers and employees **12**	Provide inviting demonstration and test rooms **22**	Ensure visitors are dealt with in a planned way **32**	Ensure accurate and timely supply of goods **42**	Ensure that signs etc. direct customers in a planned way **52**	Organise work to present a consistent approach **62**	Provide new physical environment for new work processes **72**
Secure a lasting and equitable contract **13**	Provide easy access to all customer facilities **23**	Develop a service-oriented telephone culture **33**	Offer and provide high quality maintenance agreements **43**	Put into effect a continuous improvement programme **53**	Develop required staff skills and expertise **63**	Establish clear responsibility and measures **73**
Secure the basis for a long term growth plan **14**	Provide a building which encourages staff to focus on customer service **24**	Focus staff on solving customer problems **34**	Provide a 24 hour telephone service **44**	All staff know and accept their job requirements **54**	Develop insight into work of and dependence on others **64**	Provide logistics solution which support Column 4 **74**
Work within local authority constraints and regulations **15**	Space layout which encourages tidiness **25**	Present all products with a consistent quality image **35**	Provide timely completion of technical service **45**	**55**	Develop a reward system which matches the programme's goals **65**	Devlop an IT network which helps integrate the company **75**
Ensure the building satisfies the phased space requirements **16**	Use colour and graphics for appropriate customer ambience **26**	Ensure complaints are dealt with promptly and courteously **36**	Provide customers with appropriate skills through training **46**	**56**	Develop a culture of shared prosperity through shared responsibility **66**	Develop a customer database which helps us improve service **76**
17	Segregate work areas from traffic effectively **27**	**37**	Ensure all written materials conform to quality and graphics standards **47**	**57**	**67**	Provide canteen and other services which promote teamwork **77**

Figure 10.1 *Objective Breakdown Structure for Relocation example*

The idea behind the project is to use the relocation to create a more competitive company. The objective breakdown structure should deal with all aspects of the business that possibly could be affected by the move to new premises and the measures taken to improve the company.

The objective breakdown structure shows that the basic goal of the organisation is to strengthen our market position and profitability through total management of customer service and supply in a service-oriented building. The basic goal is shown in the top box of the objective breakdown structure. Sometimes it is natural to call it the mission of an organisation.

The objective breakdown structure should further illustrate what has be done in order to make the basic goal a reality. The goal is broken down into some core objectives and some managing and supporting functions.

In our example we have identified one core objective related to the actual building, two concerning the customers (one dealing with quality in general, the other with the supply of goods and services), and finally two core objectives that have to do with the staff of the organisation and their commitment to service and their way of working. We always place the core objectives in the middle of the objective breakdown structure.

The core objective of the building is shown (column 2). All sub-objectives in this column refer to properties of the building, ie: *to have a service building which makes it easy to be our customer.* Thereafter we have the two core objectives relating to customers. It is of little use having a fine building if customers do not experience service and quality in our treatment of them (column 3) and what we deliver (column 4): *to ensure customers experience quality in all aspects of customer management,* and: *to ensure quality and accuracy in supply of goods and services.* Then there are two internal development core objectives. Staff will not act in a different and better way without specific initiatives to bring this about. There must be a commitment towards quality and service (column 5) and internal development in the form of reorganising and training (column 6): *to commit all staff through our public commitment to customers,* and: *to reorganise the work and introduce new skills.*

The objective breakdown structure will, in addition to the core objectives and their sub-objectives, also show the neccessary managing and supporting functions.

In our example we have identified one managing function. It may also be referred to as a basic precondition. It has to do with establishing the economic and physical basis for the new premises and any further expansion (column 1): *to provide financially and physically for planned and future growth.* Finally, there is a pure support function (column 7): *to introduce effective work processes and administrative support.*

This objective breakdown structure shows what the company wants to achieve in the new premises. The project will contribute to this. But the project must not necessarily take on everything itself. By using the breakdown structure it is relatively simple to define exactly what the project will be responsible for and what the base organisation will be responsible for.

When we have decided what the project will be responsible for (which objectives the project will contribute towards fulfilling), we can formulate the goals for the project. At the same time we can decide what is the line's responsibility.

PURPOSE

You have now seen an example of an objective breakdown structure and obtained an idea of the way in which it should be used. Let us look more closely at the motive for drawing it up.

An internal development project should contribute to the business functioning better in the future. The objective of such projects can always be expressed by describing what we want the future business to be. In this instance an objective breakdown structure provides an ideal vision of what the business will do. We may suppose that an insurance company will acquire a new computer-based system. The aim of this is to provide certain types of insurance services, to have flexible products, to give good customer service and to be efficient. The objective breakdown structure gives a precise picture of the insurance company's purpose for the new insurance system.

Objective breakdown structures work equally well for projects undertaken by public authorities to provide a benefit to society at large, rather than to develop the organisation. We may, for example, consider an extensive road-building project. The core objectives that will be taken into consideration may be good accessibility, high traffic safety, acceptable noise and pollution, rational use of space, positive landscape impact and minimum use of resources.

Work on an objective breakdown structure should result in:

❑ Everyone involved having a common understanding of what the project is for.
❑ People having a complete picture of all the objectives and functions that may be considered to be included in the project.
❑ A clear demarcation that defines what the project is responsible for and what it is not responsible for (ie what others are responsible for).
❑ Setting qualitative and quantitative goals for the project.

The purpose of the objective breakdown structure is thus to create a precise picture of what contribution the project will make to the development of the business or its environment. This will create a common understanding of the purpose of the project and its scope. At the same time, it will show what the project will not do. This shows what others, especially the line, must do in order for it to be possible to realise all the objectives contained within the breakdown structure.

DEVELOPMENT OF AN OBJECTIVE BREAKDOWN STRUCTURE

Practical experience has taught us that it is sensible to standardise the design of the objective breakdown structure – but obviously not the content. Figure 10.2 shows a form which can be used for this.

We start with a heading which expresses the basic goal (mission) upon which the whole objective breakdown structure is built. Under the basic goal we organise the core objectives

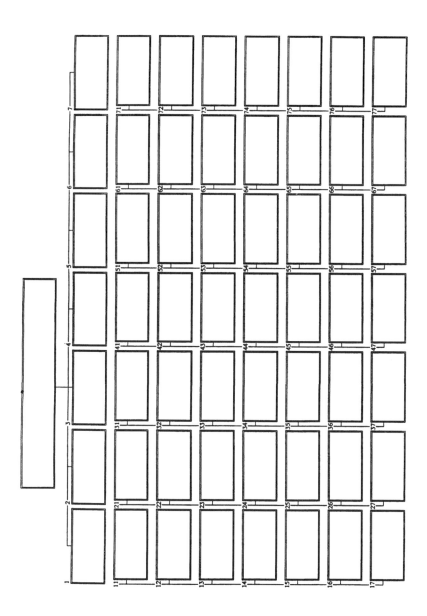

Figure 10.2 *The proforma for the objective breakdown structure*

and the managing and supporting functions in a maximum of seven columns. Each column has a main heading, with a maximum of seven boxed sub-divisions.

We use the middle columns for the core objectives, which it should be possible to derive from the basic idea. The left-hand columns are reserved for managing (prerequisite) functions. These are functions which are essential if the core objectives are to be achieved. The column(s) to the right are reserved for support functions. The core objective in one column (level 2) is divided into sub-objectives (level 3).

It is important to work on and develop the structure. There should be as few grey areas between the columns as possible. If you have continual placement problems, it means that the headings should be moved or adjusted.

The descriptions are important and worth formulating carefully. It is often difficult to formulate the top-level objective, the basic idea, and easy to obtain descriptions which are long but unhelpful. The objective breakdown structure is a means of communication, so it should communicate accurately. The choice of verbs may be important; there is a significant difference between words such as 'develop', 'secure' and 'acquire', for example.

The objective structure often provides the basis for a significantly improved milestone plan and may suggest good choices for result paths, as well as ensuring thorough coverage of all dimensions of the project. Finally, the detailed consideration and discussion required to develop it may provide new ideas and new insights.

The method of approach for developing the objective breakdown structure is similar to the one we recommend for work on the milestone plan. It is essentially a group task, but the group must not be too large. Eight people is probably the upper limit. The group leader needs to organise the process in advance but other participants need only come fresh and free from other demands on their time.

The group room will require an overhead projector, a whiteboard and a flipchart. A full day should normally be set aside. It may be appropriate to present a preliminary structure back to others in the organisation for comment and then resume work, say, a week later.

The process itself is simple:

- ❏ Show the objective breakdown structure proforma on the white-board.
- ❏ Begin with the basic goal (mission) and discuss the key elements.
- ❏ Try different formulations. When the group has agreed on a usable starting point, write the formulation with a non-permanent pen on the board.
- ❏ Enter keywords in the structure and headings for the lower levels.
- ❏ Draw up proposed texts for these.
- ❏ Adjust the basic goal if necessary.
- ❏ Continue column by column to find a structure for the lower levels.
- ❏ Draw up the text.

The reason for using a white-board is that we can make changes easily, and that it is a work form which facilitates effective group work. It takes from one to three days, depending on its complexity, to develop an objective breakdown structure which is good enough for further work.

In this further work, the objectives will be elaborated and explained in further detail and their relative importance evaluated and compared. How well the objectives are met at present may also be considered. This will set the priorities for and determine the scope of the project itself which, we emphasise again, will not normally embrace the whole objective breakdown structure.

11

Conclusion

Before we finish we would like to show that tools and techniques from GDPM can also be used in other fields. We will also offer some advice regarding the connection between project work and business certification. We will see whether GDPM satisfies the 'requirement specification' which we presented in Figure 3.6. We will conclude with some good advice.

GOAL DIRECTED PROJECT MANAGEMENT USED IN OTHER FIELDS

The central tools of GDPM are the milestone plan and the responsibility chart. They contribute to structuring the project task and determining responsibility for its different elements.

These tools can be used in fields other than project management. Milestone plans are relevant when work progress is to be described and when the logical relationships between the different results which are to be obtained in the course of the work are to be specified. This applies, for example, to describing administrative procedures in an organisation. The responsibility chart is relevant whenever responsibilities must be made clear. This is desirable, for example, when drawing up job descriptions.

An administrative procedure often consists of developing different documents that provide information, represent a basis for decisions, and record the outcome. A purchasing procedure includes everything from identifying the current suppliers to completing the purchase. In the course of this procedure different types of work will be performed, which will result in different documents. In practice there is a logical sequence in the work and in the development of the documents.

A milestone plan and responsibility chart are good tools for describing procedures. Purely verbal descriptions of procedures easily become voluminous. The result is that the overview disappears and procedures are neither read, understood nor used. The milestone plan is effective because it focuses on results and shows the logical links between the different documents. The responsibility chart provides a precise division of roles.

When the milestone plan is used to describe a procedure, we call it a procedure plan. It can be expanded with references to manuals, supporting regulations, requirements for documents, and so on. If it is very important to ensure that the procedure is followed, the report field can be used to document results as the procedure is carried out.

We will show one example of a procedure plan for a firm of consultants which follows procedures from initial inquiry to contract (Figure 11.1).

The following were selected as result paths in the plan:

❑ the methods the firm will use, which resources it has and the resources required (MR);
❑ the assignment (AS);
❑ the client's requirements which must be satisfied (RQ);
❑ the client's resource input and other prerequisites concerning the client which must be satisfied to achieve results (RS).

The report part of the milestone plan is used to give:

❑ references to instructions (I);
❑ references to aids and supporting information (A).

An additional advantage of using tools from GDPM for describing procedures is that this way of thinking will be introduced throughout the organisation. Everyone will become familiar with milestone plans and responsibility charts.

MILESTONE PLAN

From an inquiry to a contract

Project description	Approved by/Date — Project Manager
Potential client's inquiry registered and the responsibility for handling the request has been assigned to a consultant and scope of quality assurance is agreed upon	I: Procedures for handling requests to tender
We have decided whether to tender or not based on our general experience and resource situation	I: Procedures for handling requests to tender; A: Prerequisites for the tender
We have acquired the necessary additional professional and formal information in order to submit a serious offer (incl. understanding the client's need)	A: Checklist
The tender's form, structure and content are finalised, including a breakdown of the assignment into phases when necessary	I: Local standards; A: Checklists, Previous tenders, Standard tender
Methods, qualification requirements, team composition including actual consultants decided upon	I: Local standards; A: Survey of qualifications, Previous similar assignments
The assignment's different elements estimated, uncertainty and risks areas identified, quality requirements identified	I: Local standards; A: Estimating techniques
Necessary input from the client in order to get results (resource input etc.) is specified and as far as possible quantified	I: Local standards
Offer to carry out an assignment (AS2) creating results for the client (RQ4) based on the client's as well as our effort (RS2, MR3) is submitted in writing. Internal quality assurance carried out according to procedure	I: Procedures for tendering; A: Standard tender
We have been notified that a) we lost the assignment, b) the decision has been deferred	
We have been notified that we won the assignment. Confirm in writing if the message is verbal	I: Procedures for contract handling
We have been notified that the client wishes to finalise the contract	I: Procedures for contract handling
Consultants to work on the project have been selected and committed in time and mandays	I: Procedures for contract handling
Contract signed, including how the assignment is to be carried out (AS6), results to be produced for the client (RQ5), methods, people, costs and prerequisites (MR5) and the client's input and quality assurance (RS3)	I: Procedures for contract handling

Column headings (logic network):

Planned date	Our methods & resources — MR	Assignment — AS	Client's requirements — RQ	Client's resources — RS
			RQ1	RS
			RQ2	
			RQ3	
		AS1		RS1
	MR1			
	MR2			
	MR3	AS2	RQ4	RS2
		AS3		
		AS4		
		AS5		
	MR4			
	MR5	AS6	RQ5	RS3

Figure 11.1 *The milestone plan used to describe the procedure 'From an inquiry to a contract'*

ISO 9000 CERTIFICATION AND PROJECT MANAGEMENT

There is increasing interest throughout Europe in applying quality control and obtaining formal quality certification. We will examine more closely the consequences of this for project work.

ISO 9000 is a standard for quality management and quality assurance. It consists of several elements. ISO 9001 to 9003 are requirement standards. They describe the bases on which a company can be certified. (9001–9003 differ from each other in that they cover different parts of a company.) ISO 9004 is a set of guidelines that can be used when setting up a quality system within a company.

A company can decide for itself what it wants to have certified – the whole company or parts of it. For example, it is possible to have only the research and development department certified.

More and more companies will be required to have ISO certification in order to be able to become national or international suppliers. This applies equally in manufacturing, commerce and the service industry.

In order to discuss certification in more detail it is necessary to recognise at least one concept from the standards. This is a 'quality system'. It stands for 'organisational structure, responsibility, procedures, processes and resources in implementation of quality management'.

How then does project management fit in with this? It does so in two ways.

First, a company may wish to be certified and may start a development programme to improve its quality system. The development programme must consist of a series of development projects – PSO projects. It appears to take from one to two years to develop a quality system good enough for certification. If the company is to be successful in working out a good quality system, it must emphasise heavily quality in the development projects. The company will need to take seriously all the factors of project culture and quality we discussed earlier.

Secondly, project management can be included as part of the company's certificated quality system. This is relevant in cases where the project work form is an essential part of the company's method for producing results for customers. This can apply to a construction company, a firm of consultants which uses projects in cooperation with customers, a research organisation which does contract research, and so on. Then good project management not only helps to improve the company; project management is a part of the company's quality system which will be inspected during certification. This demands even more from project management. All the factors from Chapters 8 and 9 obviously still apply, but in addition, the requirements for documentation are even more stringent, because it should be possible for an external certification agency to see that project management has been performed 'by the book'.

As a minimum, the following matters must be documented in project work:

- Project description and justification with goals and result requirements.
- Division of the project with descriptions and estimates.
- Milestone plans and responsibility charts.
- Phase evaluation.
- Project evaluation.

The certification agency will not assess the quality of milestone plans and responsibility charts, for example. It will only ascertain whether the documentation exists. The fact remains, however, that a company will have problems implementing the project if quality is poor.

ISO 9000 certification will be important in the future, whether project work is part of the quality system or not. Therefore we end this section with an example of a milestone plan (Figure 11.2) and a responsibility chart (Figure 11.3) for a certification project. In this case certification was sought by a technological company with fewer than 50 employees.

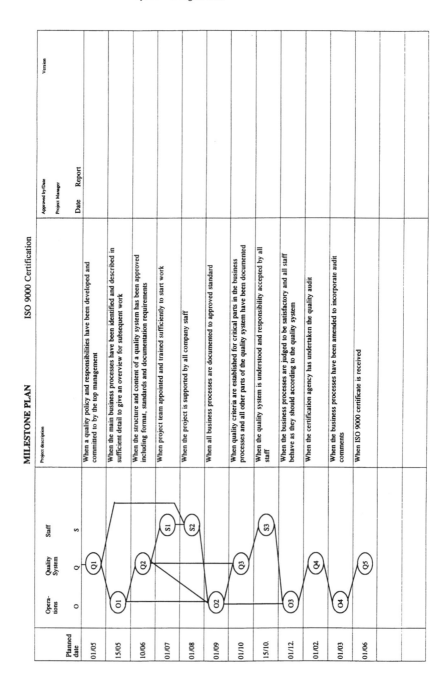

Figure 11.2 *Milestone plan for a quality certification project*

PROJECT RESPONSIBILITY CHART   **ISO 9000 Certification**

Legend:
- X - executes the work
- D - takes decision solely
- d - takes decision jointly
- P - manages progress
- T - provides tuition on the job
- C - must be consulted
- I - must be informed
- A - available to advise

* Quality Manager - to be appointed before milestone Q3

No.	Milestones	Compl. Date	Managing Director (1)	Management group (2)	Quality Manager* (3)	Sales (4)	Finance/administration (5)	Technical (6)	Project manager (7)	Project team (8)	ISO 9000 consultant (9)	Certification agency (10)
Q1	Quality policy	01/05	D	dX					P		A	
O1	Business processes overview	15/05				C	C	C	PX		T	
Q2	Quality system	10/06	D	d					PX		T	
S1	Basic training	01/07	I	I		I	I	I	PX	X	T	
S2	Project support	01/08	D	X					PX	X	A	
O2	Documented business processes	01/09		I	d	d	d	d	P	X	A	
Q3	Quality system supplemented	01/10	D	d	d	C	C	C	PX	X	A	
S3	Quality training	15/10		X		X	X	X	PX	T	A	
O3	System in use	01/12		I	I	X	X	X	P	A	A	
Q4	Quality audit	01/02	I		I				I			PX
O4	Quality corrections	01/03			d	X	X	X	PX		A	
Q5	ISO 9000 certification	01/06	I									PX

Estimated time (days)

Figure 11.3 *Project responsibility chart for a quality certification project*

FULFILMENT OF 'REQUIREMENT SPECIFICATION'

After discussing pitfalls in Chapter 3, we summarised in Figure 3.1 the dangers that it is particularly important to avoid. We called this figure a requirement specification. To make it easier to read we have repeated it as Figure 11.4.

- The project must work on tasks which are important for the base organisation. There should be a close correlation between the business plans and the objectives of the project

- The base organisation should have principles and policies of project work

- Project methods and tools must compel those involved to spend time on defining project objectives and goals, ie what the project should achieve

- Project methods and tools must compel those involved to focus on giving the project a composite goal, which encompasses matters relating to people, systems (technical matters) and organisation

- Project planning must take place at at least two levels

- Short-term, controllable intermediate goals must be set

- A plan must be clearly presented on a single sheet of standard-sized paper

- Those who draw up the plans must know that they themselves will have to live with the consequences of them

- There must be an understanding of the fact that change processes take time

- There must be an understanding of what control is, and how important this task is in project work

- A plan must be formulated in such a way that it both facilitates and promotes control

- The project manager must be given authority in his dealing with the base organisation
- Procedures for reporting must be established
- There must be an understanding that a project can be organised in several different ways
- The lines of responsibility in the project must be clearly described
- Binding agreements for releasing resources for the project must be drawn up
- Line management and project members should be highly motivated
- A project manager with the right qualities must be selected
- Concrete work must be done to create good conditions for cooperation in the project
- Common methods must be selected for work on the project which also encourages communication between the experts and users
- Changes in project objectives and goals must be made after careful consideration
- There must be quality control throughout the project

Figure 11.4 *'Requirement specification'– important factors for avoiding pitfalls in projects (also shown as Figure 3.1)*

In Chapter 3 we promised that after going through GDPM we would assess whether it satisfied the requirement specification. We will do so in this section by running briefly through our views on how the method meets the requirements. The points are stated below using keywords. The complete text appears in Figure 11.4.

Important tasks for the base organisation

The use of an objective breakdown structure ensures this.

Principles and policies for project work

The principle responsibility chart establishes the central principles for decision-making authority, communication, participation and division of work in the project.

Precise definition of the project's goals

The milestone plan, with its result paths, requires goals to be defined precisely. Without goals it is impossible to set up a good milestone plan.

Focusing on composite goals

This is taken care of when the milestone plan has several result paths, which show that the project should produce several types of results.

Layered planning

This is one of the strongest points of the method. Planning (and control) occurs at both global and detail levels.

Short-term controllable intermediate goals

The milestones in the milestone plan serve this function.

Clear plans

The different forms provide the framework for a clear presentation of the whole project.

The planner must live with the plan

The principle responsibility chart clarifies responsibility relationships. We have stressed that those who will perform an activity must participate in planning it.

Understanding that change takes time

The method does not have much to offer here, but division into several result paths in the milestone plan, with the opportunity to focus on human adjustment and development, provides more realistic planning of the human change processes.

Understanding control

We do not guarantee that the method will provide a deeper understanding of control, but the simple and manageable reporting procedures following certain control criteria should facilitate control.

The plans promote and facilitate control

This is a strong point of the method. The control criteria are defined precisely on plan and report forms. Conditions are correctly set up for individual reports and meaningful control.

Project manager with authority in the line

The principle responsibility chart and the project responsibility chart define precisely the terms of responsibility and authority, but this method cannot guarantee that everyone will live up to what is described and agreed upon. The formal agreement makes it easier to follow up if the line is not meeting its commitments.

Established pattern of communication

Reporting is formalised. In addition we have stressed that the deeper report dialogue should be structured and not 'idle chatter'.

Understanding that there are different ways of organising a project

The responsibility chart promotes a discussion of different ways of dividing work tasks and decisions in a project. The discussion shows that people are free to organise themselves in many different ways.

Clear descriptions of responsibility in the project

Again a strong point of the method. The responsibility chart clarifies terms of responsibility. They are precise and difficult to run away from.

Binding agreements on releasing resources

The responsibility chart is such a binding agreement.

Motivated line manager and project members

This is a matter which the method does not specifically deal with, though probably the overview and the clear agreements required by the method, and clarity of reporting and control, will aid motivation.

Correct choice of project manager

This is an area where the method does not make a significant contribution. The method starts when the project manager has been chosen.

Good cooperation in the project

Neither is this an area which the method covers in detail though it is important and methods to improve cooperation in the project should be drawn from elsewhere. We believe that clear areas of responsibility and authority are a good basis on which to build cooperation.

Methods that promote communication between users and experts

Detail planning is formalised through an activity responsibility chart. Specific methods are described, which are important with reference to both time scheduling and resource estimation. The project management method in itself does not require or stimulate use of particular methods in the professional work.

Changes in goals after careful consideration

The responsibility charts define precisely who can decide on changed goals.

Quality control along the way

The milestones make it possible to check that the project is progressing according to plan. We have stressed that the milestones should be formulated so that it is also possible to undertake quality control.

FINAL COMMENTS

We have now presented GDPM.

We have gone through the principles which are important when planning, organising and controlling projects. We have shown that GDPM is a comprehensive method which builds on these principles.

The method requires an ability to think logically and systematically through a task and to describe precisely what has been agreed upon. It is supported by certain forms. These discipline the work and make it easier to follow the method. However, there are few forms, so that the work does not become unduly complex.

A project which follows GDPM substantially improves its chances of being a successful project. However, we have also underlined the significance of the project culture for the results. Therefore it is necessary to include a reminder of this by way of conclusion. The organisation must work constantly on improving its project culture. We suggested a comprehensive and systematic projectivity programme.

Even if you do not start such a programme you can improve the project culture in the base organisation. We would therefore like to point out four areas which everyone should work on in order to improve the chances for successful projects:

The organisation must demonstrate that it wants to manage its projects

A minimum for a project management policy is that management agrees that all projects over a certain size and complexity should be planned and organised with the aid of a milestone plan and a responsibility chart.

The organisation must demonstrate that it is concerned with the progress of its projects

It is a good discipline if all projects have to submit a milestone report to the managing director (or another person in top management, if this is more appropriate) on the first day of every month.

The organisation must increase the professional prestige of project management

Project management must be regarded as a distinct profession demanding great expertise and long experience. An organisation can only have a limited number of people with the necessary qualifications. It must select workers with good organisational experience as project managers. Young, inexperienced people are too lightweight. You must invest in people who are willing to be project managers, and who do not only see this position as a short episode, a stepping stone to line management.

The organisation must make use of its own project experience and constantly develop project expertise

It is desirable that project managers have their own forum with fixed meeting times, for example the last working day of each month. Examination of project reports and discussions of new plans, with the aim of improving quality, should be permanent agenda items at such meetings. Discussing common problems must be a central point. The most usual themes will be lack of resources, slow decision-making processes, difficulties in prioritisation, and changes in priority.

Index